In the beginning was the Word, and the Word was Change.

—*A. B. GUTHRIE, JR.*

e

Big Sky, Fair Land

The Environmental Essays of

A. B. Guthrie, Jr.

Edited by David Petersen

 Northland·Press

To the spirit of Dick Summers. . .the genuine article.

Excerpts on pages 9–17 from *The Big Sky* by A. B. Guthrie, Jr. Copyright 1947 and copyright renewed 1974 by A. B. Guthrie, Jr. Reprinted by permission of Houghton Mifflin Company.

Excerpts on pages 19–28 from *The Way West* by A. B. Guthrie, Jr. Copyright 1949 by A. B. Guthrie, Jr. and copyright renewed 1976 by A. B. Guthrie, Jr. Reprinted by permission of Houghton Mifflin Company.

Excerpts on pages 29–34 from *Fair Land, Fair Land* by A. B. Guthrie, Jr. Copyright 1982 by A. B. Guthrie, Jr. Reprinted by permission of Houghton Mifflin Company.

Excerpts on pages 35–39 from *These Thousand Hills* by A. B. Guthrie, Jr. Copyright 1982 by A. B. Guthrie, Jr. Reprinted by permission of Houghton Mifflin Company.

Excerpts on pages 41–45 from *Arfive* by A. B. Guthrie, Jr. Copyright 1970 by A. B. Guthrie, Jr. Reprinted by permission of Houghton Mifflin Company.

Excerpts on pages 47–52 from *The Last Valley* by A. B. Guthrie, Jr. Copyright 1975 by A. B. Guthrie, Jr. Reprinted by permission of Houghton Mifflin Company.

4.5 M/4-88/0101-S

CONTENTS

PART II

The Environmental Essays of A. B. Guthrie, Jr.

PREFACE

On a winter's night many years ago, a father gave his teenage son a gift that would prove to be one of the treasures of the boy's life.

"Here," the father said, handing over a novel he'd just finished after a week of reading during the short hours between work and bed, "you'll go for this one."

The book's cover illustration was a soft-toned watercolor. In the foreground stood a buckskin-clad frontiersman and, kneeling nearby, a long-haired Indian girl. Behind the couple spread a raw wilderness of rolling short-grass plains snaked through with a limpid snow-melt stream. And prominent in the landscape was an odd-shaped mountain—a liberal imagination could have it looking like an ear turned on its side—looming big against the sky. The illustration wasn't really very good, but it was plenty good enough to capture the interest and imagination of a restless teenage boy. The name of the book was *The Big Sky,* and its author was A. B. Guthrie, Jr.

As my father had suggested I would, go for it I did. Most teens are anything but refined readers. I was no exception, loping along oblivious to many, if not most, of the literary nuances and subtle images warping through a tightly woven tale of freedom and danger set in a land almost too wild and grand to comprehend. I knew such a place existed, physically at least.

While I may have missed the literary and philosophical nuances of *The Big Sky* in that first, fast pursuit of its adventure, I certainly didn't miss the mystique. I was enchanted, captivated. I read the book from cover to cover, then I read it again.

Midway through the first reading I was convinced that I'd been born 150 years too late. By the end of the second read I was ready to stuff my backpack with sandwiches and a blanket and chase after the spirits of the book's two young adventurers, Caudill and Deakins, who'd followed before me the trail to the good, hard life that I was certain could still be found in those shining mountains of Guthrie's West.

Many years and many wrong trails later I managed to attain the life of my Big Sky dreams. Sort of. For several years now I have lived in a little mountain cabin high in the Rockies—not remote, but comfortably secluded. Out my door and just a short hike through the surrounding forests of spruce and aspen lies a sprawling national forest and, a little farther on, designated wilderness. Mule deer and black bears are my timid neighbors, and through the valley below perks a sparkling, snow-melt stream. From my front doorstep, with binoculars trained across the way, I watch elk graze in wildflowered meadows spring and summer, and hear them bugle come fall. Each winter, deep snows close the rutted dirt lane that climbs up to my little redoubt, leaving my wife and me to trudge the final stretch on snowshoes, carrying what we need in backpacks or dragging it on a sled. I hunt, fish, observe, explore and generally live about as close to nature as a city-bred man with limited means can manage these days.

I make no claim to be a mountain man, and Colorado in the late twentieth century is no wilderness frontier. Still, it's a good life, a dream fulfilled. And I owe its inspiration to that book my father gave me nearly 30 years ago, and to the man who imagined and penned it.

I wore out that first paperback of *The Big Sky* way back when, and have tattered three more copies—hardbound and soft—since, blemishing pages with scribbled marginalia. I have studied, written about, even taught *The Big Sky* and subsequent Guthrie novels. I have explored extensively and even lived for a short while in the geographical reality of Guthrie's fiction. And finally, in the spring of 1983, I met the man.

In 1980 I had quit my job as managing editor of a small magazine in Southern California, packed my scant possessions into my old VW bus and, with Carolyn, my spouse-to-be, made the move of my dreams. For the next three years I trapped a meager living writing magazine articles and children's books and teaching an occasional writing class at the little college in the little town of Durango, Colorado, some 15 miles down the valley from my mountain home.

After corresponding with Guthrie for more than a year, I asked him for an interview. He agreed, so as soon as school was out in the spring of '83, Carolyn and I tossed our camping gear into the back of our old pickup truck and headed north.

As we cruised slowly through Guthrie's hometown of Choteau, Montana, we marked a pleasant western village, typical of many small agricultural towns that have been spared rampant growth and its accompanying tacky modernization. A sleepy main street squared a large quarried-stone courthouse. Most of the homes and buildings were vintage and neatly kept. The small town park had a crew-cut lawn shaded by ancient cottonwoods.

Quaint. Even pleasant. Still, it was hard to imagine that the tranquil scene we were observing had served as the inspiration for Guthrie's semi-autobiographical novel *Arfive* and its sequel, *The Last Valley.* Then, off to the northwest, toward the pristine Bob Marshall Wilderness, we noted a familiar landmark, an odd-shaped mountain looking remotely like an ear turned on its side.

I phoned from the only cafe we could find open on a Sunday afternoon in Choteau, and Carol Guthrie—with the confidence and exactitude borne of having run this drill many times before—dictated directions to the place that her husband, in our correspondence, always referred to as "The Barn."

From Choteau to the Barn is some 25 country miles north and west, a good part of the way over gravel and dirt. Now and again a pheasant would flush from the roadside brush as we rattled past—a flutter, a bright multicolored flash, and gone. As we neared the end of my scribbled directions, we spotted an attractive two-story, wood house pitched on a low bench. A gravel driveway stretched across the jackpine-studded flat between road and house.

Before turning onto the drive, I stopped the truck and crawled out for a stretch and a look. The surrounding country was mostly open and rolling, flattening a bit toward the east as foothills gave way to bench-lands and, farther on, high plains. Westward, the terrain steepened sharply, with the view cut off close and clean by the north-south wall of the Rockies.

There was a ski area back up in those mountains somewhere (we'd seen the signs along the highway), sitting on national forest land, as most western ski areas do. Beyond that would be the heads of deep-worn trails that for decades had taken intrepid hikers and riders into a gigantic patch of mountain wilderness—at more than a million acres, the largest in the lower 48—that locals refer to simply as "the Bob." On the maps of ancient seafarers, unknown (and, thus, feared) regions were marked with the warning, "Here there be tygers." *Here* there be grizzlies.

Nearby the Barn, the land was peppered with gnarled jackpines and snaked through by a slow mountain stream, the Teton River, meander-ing placidly along a wide, glacier-gravel channel that looked to have been intended by nature to carry a much stronger flow.

Five miles southeast of the Barn, I knew, lay the 12,000-acre Pine Butte Swamp Preserve, owned by the Nature Conservancy, an organization devoted to the preservation of uncommon or threatened plants and animals. Among those animals are grizzly bears. In the spring after hibernation the bears are famished for green stuff, and so a few of them venture out to the swamp. Perhaps a number of them have gone farther; no one really knows. But in two recent years some grizzlies, swamp bears or not, *have* gone farther, to the outrage of two or three ranchers who have lost stock. Here, in the Choteau and Teton County area, is the only place in the West nowadays where grizzlies travel so far afield.

Off to the southwest, less than a few miles distant, rose Ear Moun-tain, its ridged crest looming near and tall, looking even more mysterious and compelling in still life than it had on the cover of that first copy of *The Big Sky* my father had given me.

I climbed back in the truck and drove on.

A smiling couple met us at the Barn's front door. The man intro-duced himself as Bud. (The nickname, I knew from having read his autobiography, was suggested inadvertently by a younger sister who, as a toddler, couldn't quite get a handle on his middle name, Bertram.)

Guthrie was thinner than I had expected from photographs on the dust jackets of his books, his slightness accentuated by heavy, dark-framed spectacles and wide suspenders. ("Can't keep a belt on a carrot," he jokes.) Still, he stood proud and straight and would prove to be everything of a gentleman. But neither was this Pulitzer-winning novelist effete; his conversation was never fearful of calling on the earthy language of a ranch hand to add spice and spine to the wide-ranging vocabulary of a Harvard fellow and recipient of two honorary doctorate degrees.

Carol Guthrie, several years younger than her husband, was trim and attractive. We would find her to be open and friendly, sophisticated yet unpretentious. Haunched down between Carol and Bud was a woolly pup the size and color of a shovelful of anthracite. With a wag of tail it answered to the name Little John.

The Guthries' energy and good cheer quickly pulled Carolyn and me past the uneasiness that so often stiffens first meetings. Carol led us through the living room, past a large open kitchen to a solarium. As we entered, I noted that the sunny room provided an unrestricted, head-on view of Ear Mountain and the blue peaks that shouldered up to its flanks.

When I commented on the view, and Carolyn on the pleasantness of the room's interior (woody and bright, the walls hung with photographs and original dust-jacket art from various novels), Guthrie was quick to credit Carol as the architect and decorator. He pointed us to a wicker couch. When we'd settled he said, "Not long before we added this room on, we looked out the window one day to see a black bear right where you're seated now."

I asked about grizzlies. (A question I was later to learn Guthrie had heard so often as to consider mundane, even silly.)

"Oh, they're out there," he said. "They use the Teton as a nighttime runway down from the mountains to the big swamp and back. But we don't see them because we don't leave garbage out to attract them. There are probably as many grizzlies in this area as anywhere in the lower 48 outside Yellowstone and Glacier parks, but we've never had a speck of trouble."

I let my vision wander out through the big, ceiling-to-floor windows. Not another house or manmade structure in sight. Just Ear Mountain, which Carol refers to as "Buddy's Mountain," looming in the near distance with plenty of open land all around, much of it dotted with the tortured-looking little jackpines that nonetheless are tough enough to have hung on for hundreds, even thousands, of years in the rocky soil and harsh climate. The Guthries' little chunk of Montana real estate, I reflected, was an uncut gem—rough-edged and unpolished to the quick and unknowing glance, its deeper beauty apparent only when turned the right way in the mind's eye. I said as much.

Guthrie laughed. "This 160 acres is so poor we can't even raise hell on it."

I thought of Guthrie and his times in Lexington, Cambridge, and Los Angeles, and I wondered if here, secluded as he was, he didn't occasionally get bored. I put the question to him.

"You have to count the advantages and disadvantages," he answered. "Sure, we miss big-city concerts and the theater and good speakers and fine libraries, but we wouldn't choose to live in a big city again. Through visits from distant friends we revive ourselves.

"We go to Choteau to shop, but don't spend much time, for we have very few close friends there. All my old and tried friends are dead."

"Our closest friends live away from here," Carol added, "and lots of them come to see us. We don't suffer from lack of company."

"And no matter where we lived," Guthrie concluded, "we never could be with all of our friends at the same time."

By and by I set up my tape recorder, dragged out my notes, and the interview began. For the next four hours I hammered through a long list of prepared questions while Guthrie responded with relaxed enthusiasm. Finally, when he sensed that I'd about reached the bottom of my bucket, he said, "Enough. Turn that damn thing off so we can just visit."

Carol brought out a good, dry, white wine, and the four of us sipped and talked easily through the rest of the afternoon. The next morning, I steered the old pickup southeast from Choteau, bound for nearby Glacier Park, then home.

Later that same year I was offered editorial work with a large national magazine in North Carolina. Tired of the freelance grind, I accepted. Reluctantly. Soon enough Carolyn and I boarded up our little cabin, stuffed a small U-Haul trailer with necessities and headed east.

As lifelong westerners, we quickly found ourselves disoriented and disheartened among those hazy Appalachian hills. From the moment we left the Rockies both Carolyn and I were agonizingly homesick. For solace I returned to Guthrie's literary West of the mind and soon found myself redreaming the Rocky Mountain dreams of my youth. After 18 months in North Carolina we could stand it no longer and packed our bags for the return trip west. And, remarkably, owing primarily to the benevolence and trust of my boss, I was allowed to bring my job home with me.

Shortly after our return to Colorado in the spring of '86, a Montana magazine contacted me about working up a biographical piece on

Guthrie. I relayed the request to Guthrie. He agreed to cooperate but suggested that perhaps it would be more interesting all the way around if, rather than merely rehashing the well-publicized details of his literary career, I were to tackle an important aspect of his life that was surprisingly little known beyond the borders of Montana: his crusade, stretching back more than half a century, for the conservation of what remains pristine in America. Being a tree hugger of the first order myself, I was excited by the idea and said so. Guthrie suggested another visit, so Carolyn and I were soon on the road again.

When we arrived at the Barn, Guthrie, now 85, was looking especially chipper and announced that, after some 65 years of heavy smoking, he'd quit cold and had been "clean" for nearly six months. This short abstinence had, he calculated, already increased his vigor by a good 10 percent.

The Guthries, Carolyn, and I began by shuffling through boxes of original typed manuscripts and magazine and newspaper clippings relating to Guthrie's conservation work. We read, sorted, and talked until midnight. It was I who grew tired first, being an early bird unaccustomed to the Guthries' night-owl routine. (A normal day for them, Carol commented as we were leaving, was late morning to well past midnight.)

It was during that second visit that Guthrie entrusted me with the original drafts of the texts of a dozen or so conservation talks he'd delivered to varied audiences in recent years. Back home, I made photocopies, mailed back the originals, and began studying the neatly typed manuscripts. Almost immediately I recognized that I'd been handed another Guthrie treasure.

Although each of the essays was unique in detail, anecdote and form, all shared certain themes, the same themes, I realized, that appear in various forms and far more subtly, as literary art, in all six of Guthrie's novels of the evolving West. *Excess via too-rapid growth* was the motif, with thematic variations that included clear-cutting, strip-mining, unwise farming and ranching practices, eager-beaver damming (in both senses of the word) of rivers, fouling of air and water, wanton extirpation and extinction of species, diminution of wildlands through haphazard and myopic development, and—at the root of it all—human overpopulation. *Excess.*

While excerpting from the texts of these speeches to compile a couple of "Guthrie speaks" pieces (for *Montana* Magazine and *The Great Outdoors*), I began mentally casting about for some way to share more of

Guthrie's eloquent and compelling environmental essays with more readers. It didn't take long to hit on the idea of collecting the speech texts (most of which had never seen print)—along with Guthrie's thematically related magazine essays, book excerpts and other socio-environmental writings—between the covers of a book. Perhaps, too, I thought, it would be fitting to research and write a detailed introductory section tracing the evolution of Guthrie's conservation conscience and tracking its various manifestations through his life and literature.

A few phone calls to publishers revealed great enthusiasm for such a project, so I presented the idea to Guthrie. He approved and agreed to review my manuscript for accuracy. And that is the story of the birth of this book.

Part I, though both biographical and analytical, is neither a complete and balanced biography nor an in-depth literary analysis. It is only and exactly what its title suggests: a tracing of the evolution and expression of environmental themes in the life and literature of A. B. Guthrie, Jr. I have kept the biographical materials collared tight to that theme, wandering only as far afield as necessary to assure a sense of chronological continuity. My reviews of Guthrie's novels, likewise, are restricted to an examination of significant socio-environmental themes and images.

Part II is the beef and bones of this book, consisting of 22 of A. B. Guthrie, Jr.'s socio-environmental essays, articles, speeches and book excerpts written from 1939 to 1987. While some mainstream environmentalists may object that the concerns of certain of these essays are dated—such as Guthrie's condemnation of James Watt and cohorts in"Here and Hereafter"—I offer the reminder that at the time Guthrie wrote these pieces, he was often walking point for platoons of critics not as quick as he to see. Moreover, the intent of this book is not to break new ground, but rather to chronicle the environmental thoughts, writings and actions of one of America's greatest literary figures.

—*David Petersen*

PART I

THE EVOLUTION
AND EXPRESSION OF
ENVIRONMENTAL
THEMES IN THE LIFE
AND LITERATURE OF
A. B. GUTHRIE, JR.

INTRODUCTION

It seems a bit ironic that the man who has focused more attention on Montana than Sitting Bull and earned for her as much acclaim with his writing as Charlie Russell did with art, the man who contributed the prideful legend "Big Sky Country" to Treasure State license plates (replacing "Prison Made"), was born not in Montana, but in Bedford, Indiana.

But then, as Alfred Bertram Guthrie Junior has himself pointed out, if you ignore the first six months of life, he is a native Montanan.

Guthrie entered the world just 12 months and 13 days into the twentieth century. In July of that same year, in a move that would shape the infant's future, A. B. Guthrie, Sr. packed his family off to the still-wild West, to a speck on the map called Choteau, Teton County, Montana, population a mere few hundred. It was Front Range country, where short-grass plains rolled up from the east to wash against the flatland benches and jackpine foothills of the northern Rocky Mountains. (In his semi-autobiographical novel *Arfive*, Guthrie recalls his father's initial impression of the plains country surrounding the railroad terminus some 30 miles from Choteau as "the perfection of nowhere, the culmination of nothing.")

This risky leap from midwestern security to a roughshod western frontier town was motivated in large part by a desire for adventure. The senior Guthrie was a college-graduated schoolman in search of challenge and a freer life. In the course of his search he applied for and won appointment as principal of Teton County's first high school.

In his "scattered" autobiography, *The Blue Hen's Chick: A Life in Context* (McGraw-Hill, 1965), Guthrie recalls his father's description of their first morning in Choteau.

> He had risen early and gone outside. The air he inhaled cheered him as no air had before. Five miles southward rose two lonely buttes. . . . All up and down the western skyline stood the great blue lift of the Rocky Mountains. Benches climbed from the valley of the Teton River and to the east leveled into flatlands that ran out of sight. Overhead—you could almost say on all sides, too—was the sky—deeper, bluer, bigger than he had ever known.
>
> He breathed the air. He looked. He heard the ring of silence. . . . He stretched his arms wide and said aloud, "By George, I'm free!"

Transported by train, stagecoach and his father's will to the recent stamping grounds of fur trappers, Blackfeet Indians and grizzly bears, young Guthrie made the best of a youth's paradise by spending every spare hour abroad on the land—hunting, fishing, observing and exploring the big wild country that would be his entire world until graduation from high school and his "fix on the universe" for all of his days. From his autobiography:

> It was fine country to grow up in. . . . There were trout in the creeks, wild ducks on the waters, prairie chickens in the buck brush, rabbits in the thickets, and all within a mile or two. Service berries ripened and, later on, chokecherries, to be eaten out of hand or picked for pies and syrups. There were swimming holes called B.V.D. or Rosy Chicken, wild flowers, birds' nests, skating places, hills for coasters. . . and everywhere was room.

From the time he was old enough to handle a gun, Guthrie found pleasure and pride in bagging wild meat for the family pot. With his father's big, 12-gauge shotgun cradled in the crook of an elbow, he coursed the streams for waterfowl—blue-winged teal, pintails, mallards, Canadian honkers—or worked the buffalo grass and brushy prairie edges for the fat wild hens that would flush, cackling, from close under foot, providing good sport for the shooter who could bring his scattergun up fast and point sure, following, following, then touch the trigger at just the right moment, feeling the hard slap of recoil against his shoulder and an instant later seeing his bird fold up in a storm of feathers and tumble home to bag.

It all was good. It was good for a country boy to spend afield those precious few hours when he wasn't bent over a book at school, inking his hands at his after-school job as a printer's devil at the *Choteau Acantha*, cutting firewood or seeing to his other chores at home. It was good to be outdoors and away from people and their noisy doings, out where he could ponder the workings of nature. Out where he could hear and see and *feel* the changing of the seasons, mark a high sharp pattern of southering geese, watch spellbound as a cutthroat trout broke the glassy surface of a calm pool to lip at a stone fly and then mark the little waves washing out in concentric circles from where the insect had been. And, most of all, it was good to feel that he was a part of nature rather than apart from it.

And when the young hunter returned home successful, as he often did, it was good to see the smiles on his parents' faces and to know that he was contributing to the family weal, even if it meant killing the wild birds and animals he so admired. Even though game was plentiful in those days, Guthrie was not without misgiving. Decades later he recalled in a personal letter that "sometimes I felt sad at taking life, and I tried not to think about the wounded birds that escaped my detection and were left to die in misery. And whenever I killed bird or rabbit, I stroked feather or fur and thought how beautifully wrought the kill was."

Still, young Guthrie would continue to hunt, for his family was large and almost poor, and the cook pot always hungry. But gradually, through the years, watching came to supplant the killing in his life. Looking back, he would one day note that "the watcher lives to see watched things again, and while life maybe isn't precious, to put an end to it is mournful."

Bud Guthrie enjoyed a warm family life, scarred only by recurring sibling mortality. Of nine children, six died young. His mother, June, was educated, loving and rumored around Choteau to be "the worst housekeeper, the best cook, and the most indulgent parent known." His father was by turns sensitive and severe, quick to anger though never physically violent with his family and, at the core, always caring. The senior Guthrie took great pleasure, for instance, in passing along to his boys—Bud and his younger brother Charles ("Chick")—his love for trouting the clear waters of the Teton, angling always and only with hand-tied flies.

Well before Guthrie was old enough to handle a gun, fishing and camping with his father and brother had introduced him to the pleasures of the outdoors and the wonders of nature. As a fishing guide and fly-casting instructor, the elder Guthrie excelled. No matter the season or water conditions, he could be relied on to divine the holding places and favored foods of spunky native cutthroats. Unhampered by the formal bowtie ever-present at his collar, Abe Guthrie could make consistently flawless presentations of Professors (his favorites), Royal Coachmen and other wet-fly patterns. It was a poor fishing day indeed when the three Guthries didn't fill their creels from the holes of the Teton and its tributary creeks.

And there were other early pleasures in the outdoors. With the aid of vintage field glasses and a guide to western birds, Bud and his father spotted and identified dozens of species, some conspicuously rare thereabouts. From *The Blue Hen's Chick:*

> We counted the Savannah sparrow, the olive-backed thrush, a brown thrasher that forsook ancestral acres in favor of the West and staked a homestead in a blueberry bush. We rejoiced at seeing these and others, at knowing more about the world around us. A weakened waxwing grew into a pet. So did a redpoll, and, when spring came on, a cottontail that at first my hand would hold. I found a mallard's nest and put the eggs beneath a hen, which followed her confused brood along an irrigation ditch and was not seen again.

For Alfred Bertram Guthrie, Jr., studying and working hard and roaming wide under the clear skies of a still-fresh West, the days of youth were by turns harsh and halcyon.

In the fall of 1919, with high school behind him, Guthrie hitched horse to wagon and, accompanied by his family, drove the 20 miles to the iron tracks of the Great Northern's Oriental Limited. There he said his good-byes and boarded the whistle-stopped train, bound for Seattle and the University of Washington.

Like many, if not most, college freshmen, Guthrie didn't much care for having been so suddenly and completely separated from the familiar things of his youth—hunting, fishing, the great open spaces, friends and, most of all, his mother. And he cared even less for Seattle. ("Both the city and the campus were too big and busy," he explains, "and the sun rarely made a show.")

Thus, at the end of his first year at Seattle, Guthrie transferred his credits to the University of Montana at Missoula. In that "happier place" he would spend the next three years—learning his lessons, learning to feel at home away from home, learning who he was and who and what he wanted to become.

It was also during those years that Guthrie shucked off the last vestiges of the fundamentalist Methodism imposed by his parents, declaring himself both agnostic and liberal. (He later observed that "rebel" perhaps would have been a more befitting description.) Charles Hood, in his unpublished master's thesis titled *Hard Work and Tough Dreaming: A Biography of A. B. Guthrie, Jr.* (submitted in 1969 to the University of Montana, where he is now Dean of the School of Journalism), discussed Guthrie's college-era transformation.

> He read and appreciated Henry L. Mencken, the man who a few years later would use his cynical brilliance to poke fun at fundamentalism during the Scopes Trial in Tennessee. . . .
>
> He found meaning in the writings of naturalist John Burroughs and "forsaking Methodism, half-embraced a pantheistic faith and found defense against despair in declarations like 'The longer I live the more my mind dwells on the beauty and wonder of the world.' . . ."
>
> The years have not changed his mind. "If I have any religion," he said, "I think it is compassion, which is not supernatural at all."

But the wounds of Guthrie's fundamentalist upbringing cut deep, the scars apparent not just in his autobiography, but in the pages of many of his novels as well.

In 1923, Guthrie received an A.B. degree in journalism. Thus "enamored, neurotic and graduated," he set out to earn his way and make his mark in the world of newspaper journalism.

After searching around Montana for a while, Guthrie came to realize that locating rewarding newspaper work would necessitate exploration beyond the borders of his home state. Most of the Montana papers of the day were either too small to offer a secure future or were owned by the Anaconda Copper Company—an industrial giant whose self-promoted reputation for benevolent paternalism he seriously questioned. Even then—young, green, sorely in need of work and anxious to begin a career—Guthrie refused to join forces with anyone or anything he saw as being an enemy of nature and humanity.

So began a job-hunting odyssey that would lead the searcher as far afield as California, Old Mexico and New York. Only in July 1926, after spending the better part of two hard years on the road, did Guthrie find what he was after, hiring on as a cub reporter for the *Lexington Leader*. There he would invest his next 21 years, eventually becoming executive editor.

In 1935, Guthrie encountered in the course of his wide-ranging reading the first of two books that would affect him strongly and abide in his memory as significant influences in the formation and solidification of his environmental attitudes. The book was *Deserts on the March*, by Paul B. Sears. (The second, published in 1948, was *Our Plundered Planet*, by Fairfield Osborn.)

In Guthrie's memory, an important event of those years came on New Year's Day of 1939 when the *Leader* published his editorial decrying a local event that to other reporters was no more than marginally newsworthy, if that—the wanton killing of a golden eagle. This essay ("On the Death of an Eagle" in Part II) was A. B. Guthrie, Jr.'s first direct, written plea for the conservation of natural resources.

Beginning in the autumn of 1944, Guthrie took a year's leave of the *Leader* and moved the family he had built through the years—his wife, Harriet, their son, Alfred Bertram III ("Bert"), and daughter, Helen—to Cambridge, Massachusetts. There, as a Nieman Fellow, he would study at Harvard University.

The prestigious Nieman Fellowship had been established in 1938 "to promote and elevate the standards of journalism." Guthrie's 1944–45 group numbered nine proven journalists, he being the eldest at 43. In addition to his official program of studies in international affairs, Guthrie elected to undertake a major work of fiction.

During his nine months at Harvard (and immediately after, three more spent at the Bread Loaf Writer's Conference), writing under the guidance of Professor Theodore Morrison, Guthrie would continue the novel he had begun several months before—a fictional history of the early 1800s fur-trade era. Some three years later, at the literal last minute before going to press, the work would take on the name of *The Big Sky*. (Though widely acclaimed as his first novel, *The Big Sky* was actually Guthrie's second, the premiere effort having been a cow-country mystery titled *Murders at Moon Dance*—a work Guthrie dismisses today as a necessary but inconsequential-at-best first effort. His favorite one-word synopsis of the book is "trash.")

In 1983, at the Barn, I asked Guthrie how he came to conceive the idea of writing a mountain-man novel, which was hardly the literary vogue in the mid-1940s.

"My father," he began, "was always interested in the history of the West, and I suppose I inherited that interest. But as I got older it occured to me that a true story of the mountain man had never been told in fiction. The ones that were extant all heroized him, romanticized him. I wanted to show him for what he was, with his unworthy qualities alongside the worthy. I wanted to tell the true story. With that in mind, I did an immense amount of research. I did so much research that I almost had to take notes on my notes."

Prominent among the mountain man's "unworthy qualities," Guthrie felt, was the rapidity and thoroughness with which he had destroyed the very life he'd hied to the mountains to enjoy. In the span of less than half a century—beginning with the expedition of Lewis and Clark in 1804 and ending before 1850 (the heart's-blood years were a mere 16, those of the great fur-trade rendezvous, 1825 to 1840)—the mountain men managed to do themselves in. They trapped-out the beaver. They took most of the fight out of the fiercest Indians with the innocent introduction of smallpox and the less-than-innocent introduction of rotgut trade whisky. And they established the trails that opened the western lands to settlement and exploitation. In short, simply by living the wide-open life they loved, the mountain men—albeit unknowingly—helped to destroy it.

Such is the premise of *The Big Sky:* Man tends to destroy the things he cherishes.

In a short piece titled "The Historical Novel," which appeared in the Autumn 1954 issue of *Montana: The Magazine of Western History*, Guthrie discussed how he came to embrace this theme.

It occurred to me, as I worked at the idea, that another universal entered here, the universal of Oscar Wilde and "The

Ballad of Reading Gaol." Each man kills the thing he loves. No men ever did it more thoroughly or in shorter time than the fur hunters. . . .

In *The Big Sky*, a monumental novel of paradise found and lost, A. B. Guthrie, Jr. proved himself a master of the literary technique of foreshadowing—the subtle and artful presaging of events yet to unfold. In Guthrie's case, they unfold not just in the pages of *The Big Sky*, but incrementally throughout the six-novel saga of westering that he would author during the next 35 years.

THE

BIG

SKY

In his soundly researched Guthrie biography, Charles Hood quotes several passages from Dayton Kohler's thoughtful and balanced review of *The Big Sky*. Under the title "A. B. Guthrie, Jr. and the West," Kohler's review originally appeared in the February 1951 number of *The English Journal*. In part, Kohler says:

> We can make no greater demand upon the art of the novelist than this: Granted the imaginative reality of his story, he must convey upon the level of significant meaning some truth about human conduct and its consequences. Because Guthrie tries to answer this demand, his novel has moral value beyond mere entertainment.

Again, "he must convey. . . some truth about human conduct and its consequences." For A. B. Guthrie, Jr. in his novel *The Big Sky*, that truth is this: Man tends to destroy the very thing he most cherishes.

This message—which provides the literary premise of *The Big Sky* as well as what can be considered a cornerstone environmental theme in Guthrie's life and writing—is delivered in the novel by three major and two secondary characters.

The character of primary viewpoint—neither "protagonist" nor "antagonist" is a totally appropriate tag—is Boone Caudill. Antisocial, contrary, volatile and vengeful, Boone is a "headlong" young man of 17 at the novel's opening in 1830, a product of backwoods Kentucky. Boone is quick to act and belated in consideration of consequence and alternatives.

Boone's unlikely partner, Jim Deakins, is some 10 years older, with a diametrically opposing character. The red-haired Deakins is easygoing, sociable, better educated than Boone and thoughtful almost to the point of intellectualism.

Together, Caudill and Deakins provide *The Big Sky* with fresh young eyes that see the upper Missouri country—today's Montana—as unspoiled and ripe with opportunity and challenge.

The young partners' mentor in the ways of the mountains is Dick Summers—in his early 30s, gray of eye, wise and cool. Summers has accumulated years of experience trapping beaver, eluding and fighting Indians, and adventuring across the Rockies by the time he meets and takes the two young greenhorns in tow. Though far from jaded, Summers has been around long enough to have seen—and to have unintentionally helped bring about—the beginning of the end of the wild West.

At the opening of the novel, Summers is already feeling old, troubled by an uneasy nostalgia, as if his best years had escaped with no chance of ever being recaptured. At the heart of Summers's sadness—though he is reluctant to admit it, even to himself—is the knowledge that not just he, but the land itself has already seen its wildest, freest days. Summers and the land he loves are aging together.

Still, because he knows there's some life left in the both of them, he has bought in as part-owner of the keelboat *Mandan*. Laden with Indian trade goods and with Summers, Caudill and Deakins as the only Americans among a large French crew, the *Mandan* puts out for the upper Missouri—poling, rowing and towing every mile of the way against the heavy current, as if the great river were doing her best to stay her suitors' advances.

Thus, the character of Dick Summers ("untroubled by regrets or ambition") provides *The Big Sky's* most informed and objective viewpoint.

Although feeling both nostalgic for the good times past and uncertain about the future, Summers is satisfied to enjoy a good-enough present.

Just as Joseph Conrad, in his masterful novelette *Heart of Darkness*, employed a metaphor-laden river passage to advance the character of his protagonist narrator simultaneously with that of the darkly mysterious antagonist Kurtz, Guthrie uses the *Mandan's* upstream journey to develop his human characters simultaneously with the mystery of the great land awaiting them at their destination—the largely unexplored country above the mouth of the Yellowstone River, heart of the Blackfeet Nation.

Expectation begins building almost as soon as the *Mandan* puts out.

> Boone hitched himself closer. "It's fair country up there, I reckon."
> Summers looked at him, and his mouth made a small smile. "Wild. Wild and purty, like a virgin woman . . . there's nothin' richer'n the upper Missouri. Or purtier. I seen the Great Falls and traveled Maria's River, dodgin' the Blackfeet, makin' cold camps and sometimes thinkin' my time was up, and all the time livin' wonderful, loose and free's ary animal. That's some, that is."
> "Lord God!"

But the bright dream casts a dark shadow. A short time into the journey, some ways upstream of St. Louis, in country still rich and wild not that long ago, Summers bemoans the sudden lack of game.

> "I be dogged! I will, now. Just one deer so fur and a taste of turkey." He shook his head. "Settlers are doin' for 'em."

And a little farther on:

> "It beats all," he said, while Jim sat down on a fallen log, "how game pulls back one year after another."

Thus, even as Guthrie, through Summers's narration, provides glimpses of the pristine paradise waiting upstream, he also reminds us what becomes of wilderness when man invades it in significant numbers.

Throughout his time in *The Big Sky*, the character of Jim Deakins is Guthrie's needle for pricking the tenets of fundamentalist Christianity, in particular the concept of an anthropocentric creation—the idea that God created the world specially for man, to use and abuse as he pleases.

"Worse'n chiggers," Jim said, "these damn gnats. . . . They don't serve no purpose, unless to remind a man he ain't such a somebody. . . . Maybe the pesky little bastards is asking themselves what God wanted to put hands on a man for. . . . Maybe they're thinkin' everything would be slick, except their dinner can slap 'em. . . . Maybe they got as much business here as we have. . . . I bet they figure we're made special for them. I bet they're sayin' thank you, God, for everything, only why did You have to put hands on a man, or a tail on a cow?"

A fourth character of significant import appears only briefly. Nonetheless, Uncle Zeb Calloway stars in a pivotal scene and is central to the literary premise and socio-environmental themes of the novel.

A brother to Boone's mother, it was Uncle Zeb's brief, once-only and long-ago visit to the Caudill's Kentucky homestead that kindled the fires of wanderlust in Boone's young imagination. The next time Boone sees his uncle is in 1830, when the *Mandan* puts in at Fort Union, near the mouth of the Yellowstone.

By now Uncle Zeb is an old-timer by mountain reckoning—perhaps 60. Already a long-experienced mountain man when Dick Summers came on the scene, alcoholism and a declining market for beaver have reduced Uncle Zeb to hunting meat for the fort, trading his frontier skills for whisky. In so doing, he is creating his own tragedy by assisting the very evil he so loudly decries—the peopling of the upper Missouri. Uncle Zeb's bloodshot eyes see only the past, viewing the best years as already gone and the rest going fast—not unlike himself.

In bringing together at Fort Union these three diverse viewpoints—the eager greenness of the young partners Caudill and Deakins, the experience and balance of Dick Summers and the jaded resignation of old Zeb Calloway—Guthrie assembles the ingredients for a classic scene of literary foreshadowing. Addressing Zeb, Summers opens the dialogue.

"Caudill and Deakins, here, aim to be mountain men."
"Huh! They better be borned ag'in."
"How so?"
"Ten year too late anyhow." Uncle Zeb's jaw worked on the tobacco. "She's gone, goddam it! Gone!"
"What's gone?" asked Summers. . . .
"The whole shitaree. Gone, by God, and naught to care savin' some of us who seen 'er new." He took the knife from his belt

and started jabbing at the ground with it, as if it eased his feelings. He was silent for a while.

"This was man's country onc't. Every water full of beaver and a galore of buffler any ways a man looked, and no crampin' and crowdin'. Christ sake! . . ."

Summers' gray eye slipped from Boone to Uncle Zeb. "She ain't sp'iled, Zeb," he said quietly. "Depends on who's lookin'."

"Not sp'iled! Forts all up and down the river, and folk everywhere a man might think to lay a trap. And greenhorns comin' up, a heap of 'em—greenhorns on every boat, hornin' in and sp'ilin' the fun. Christ sake! Why'n't they stay to home? Why'n't they leave it to us as found it? By God, she's ours by rights. . . .

"Look," he said, straightening a little, "another five year and there'll be naught but coarse fur, and it goin' fast. You, Boone, and you, Deakins, stay here and you'll be out on the prairie, hide huntin', chasin' buffler and skinnin' 'em, and seein' the end come to that, too."

"Not five year," said Summers. "More like fifty."

"Ahh! The beaver's nigh gone now. Buffler's next. Won't be even a goddam poor bull fifty years ahead. You'll see plows comin' across the plains, and people settin' out to farm. . . ."

Boone heard his own voice, sounding tight and toneless. "She still looks new to me, new and purty. . . ."

"We're pushin' on," said Summers, "beyant the Milk, to Blackfoot country."

And so they do, to country so rich, thinks Boone, that a man could "kill a buffalo every day and not half try and take just the best of it and leave the rest to the wolves."

That was the way of whites new to the western mountains, seeing spread before them such a plentitude that its end was beyond their imagining. Sure, go on, take just the best and leave the rest for the wolves.

(And so they did. By the late 1840s, in *Fair Land, Fair Land*, Boone Caudill—he to whom less than two decades before the West had been "new and purty"—would find himself reduced to slaughtering buffalo for their hides; both the beaver and the market for their pelts had gone the way of history. And by 1880—the half-century predicted by Summers back in 1830 at Fort Union—Lat Evans, the protagonist of *These Thousand Hills*, will for a while attempt to earn a living in Montana Territory by poisoning wolves for the price of *their* hides. And before long even the night music of the wolves disappears, leaving only cattle and their keepers to roam beneath the big sky. And these, too, in their turn, will before long be crowded by sodbusters and they in their turn by industry, cities and as many people as a mere century before there had been beaver, buffalo and wolves. Foreshadowing. Zeb Calloway had it all pretty well figured—even if he was pushing things by a handful of decades.)

By 1837, even Boone Caudill recognizes, admits to and begins complaining of the changing face of the western land. Already the grand way of life he'd only just found looks to be waning. Many of the old-time mountain men are dead while others—Dick Summers soon to join their number—are pulling out for easier lives in the settlements. Even for a turtle of a man like Boone there is no escaping the hurtful truth that he and his fellow mountain men are a large part of the fault.

> They had hurt the hunting. . . pushing up every trickle of water until there was hardly a place a man could feel was fresh any more.

Time runs always forward, for better and for worse. And so it is that Dick Summers, feeling old in himself though little more than 40 in years, retires to a Missouri farm. Jim and Boone—still young to the West and it to them—push farther into the wilderness, eventually settling in the valley of the Teton River, in the heart of Blackfeet country. In Jim Deakins's view:

> The eye could follow the river winding and see where canyons notched the blue mountains. One peak looked like an ear turned on its side. . . . It was a place a man could spend his whole life in and never wish for better.

Along the unspoiled Teton and its tributaries—protected from exploitation by earlier fur hunters by the fierce Piegan tribe—Boone and Jim trap beaver and mink and trade their catch at Fort Benton for what little it will bring in a declining fur market, eat the good rich meat of buffalo and live with and as Indians. But change is ever approaching.

> When Jim came back from a trip he was full of talk about new forts along the river and new people moving out from the settlements and the farmers in Missouri palavering about Oregon and California, as if the mountains were a prime place for plows and pigs and corn. When Jim went on too long that way Boone

cut him off, not wanting to be bothered with fool talk that stirred a man up inside.

But Jim continues to report to Boone what he sees and hears on his excursions.

"Folks everywhere talk about Oregon and California. They aim to make up parties."

"What for?"

"To get to new land, Boone. To get where there's room to breathe, I reckon."

New land. Room to breathe. The very dreams which, only a decade before, had drawn the young partners west themselves—and Dick Summers before them, and earlier still Uncle Zeb Calloway, he following in the still-fresh tracks of Lewis and Clark.

New land, room to breathe, attracting men the likes of Elisha Peabody, the final character of significance to the environmental themes of *The Big Sky*. Peabody is a rotund Yankee entrepreneur who hires Boone and Jim to guide him over Maria's Pass—a mountain crossing he hopes one day to clear of downfallen timber and make fit for wagon travel, thus establishing a short northern toll road to Oregon. But this serious-minded easterner is driven by more than mere selfish dreams of personal wealth and greatness. Elisha Peabody is Manifest Destiny personified. As he struggles to explain to Boone:

"It is development I'm interested in, future development. You appear to think, because the Indians haven't made use of this great western country, that nobody can."

"They live in this country. They live off of it, and enj'y themselves and all," Boone answered. "What in hell do you want. Christ Almighty!"

Peabody took a deep breath, as if to make sure he had wind enough for his argument. "When country which might support so many actually supports so few, then, by thunder, the inhabitants have not made good use of the natural possibilities." His wide eyes looked at Boone, earnest and polite but not afraid. "That failure surely is justification for invasion, peaceful if possible, forcible if necessary, by people who can and will capitalize on opportunity."

"I say it's all fool talk."

"If you live, you will realize how wrong you are. Can't you see? We are growing. The nation is pushing out. . . . By every reasonable standard the land is ours—by geography, contiguity, natural expansion. Why, it's destiny, that's what it is—inevitable destiny."

Just so.

With the mountain man's way of life all but dead, here stands a well-meaning representative of the new order. An order of men with high motives who would do just as the old order had. . .chop, chew and swallow the rich feast of the West.

New land. Room to breathe.

By 1843, in the closing chapters of *The Big Sky*, Caudill, jaded and confused, returns to the settlements. But it is not so much a returning, really, as another leaving behind.

Arriving by pirogue at Independence, Missouri Territory, Caudill accosts a party of pioneers making ready for the long haul overland to Oregon by Conestoga wagon. Boone vents his considerable spleen on an unfortunate one of their number with words and tone ringing like echoes from the past:

> "You got no business in Oregon."
> "No?"
> "No more'n these others, the goddam fools! Ought to stay home and not spoil a country as wasn't meant for the likes of you."

By and by, Boone goes to visit Dick Summers. As the two old friends sit and drink and talk on Summers's porch, Boone siezes yet another opportunity to unload his pain and anger on a westering immigrant, a traveler who comes to Summers hoping to buy draft animals.

> "It ain't your country, nor any greenhorn's country. Why'n't you stay to home?"
> "I reckon there's room for all."
> Boone got up. "There ain't. She's crowded now so's a man can't catch his breath. It belongs to them as found it and lived in it. Hear?"

In his eloquent foreword to *The Big Sky*, Wallace Stegner notes:

Bigness, distance, wildness, freedom, are the dream that pulls Boone Caudill westward into the mountains, and the dream has an incandescence in the novel because it is also the dream that Bud Guthrie grew up on. . . .

The big plains and the surging ranges and the hidden valleys are a fit setting for [Guthrie's] story of intractable liberty and violence; and in the end they turn out to be not only a setting and a theme, but also, like Caudill himself, victim. The West of *The Big Sky* is Innocence, anti-civilization, savage and beautiful and doomed. . . .

In the novel's closing paragraphs, Dick Summers attempts to put the changing West into focus—for himself as much as for Boone.

"It's all sp'iled, I reckon, Dick. The whole caboodle."

"I don't guess we could help it," Summers answered, nodding. "There was beaver for us and free country and a big way of livin', and everything we done it looks like we done against ourselves and couldn't do different if we'd knowed. We went to get away and to enj'y ourselves free and easy, but folks was bound to foller and beaver to get scarce and Injuns to be killed or tamed, and all the time the country gettin' safer and better known. We ain't seen the end of it yet, Boone, not to what the mountain man does against hisself. Next thing is to hire out for guides and take parties acrost and sp'ile the country more. . . . It's like we heired money and had to spend it, and now it's nigh gone."

Nigh gone. And the mountain man working still against himself: Caudill and Deakins having aided the expansionist Elisha Peabody by guiding him to and across a northern route to Oregon. And good old Dick Summers, as yet unawares, but himself about to pilot a wagon train of eastern emigrants through the southern reaches of his old haunts, helping to people the West.

THE
WAY
WEST

Ihe sudden and indisputable success of *The Big Sky* following its release in 1947 prompted Guthrie, now 46, to retire from newspaper work. Twenty-one years was enough, he had come to feel, of racing against daily deadlines.

"Frankly," he told me, "I got tired of journalism. And I wasn't going anyplace; I'd gone as high as I could in Lexington. Newspaper writing gets to be so repetitious. All of the seasons keep rolling around, and you've got special issues and special stories that always roll around with them— the beginning of school, the end of school, Bible camp, Labor Day, Christmas, Easter. You're always looking for a new angle, a new grasp on it. I was ready for something else."

That "something else" was the novel and its attendant creative freedom. From *The Blue Hen's Chick*:

Book-publishing! Have something to say and say it well enough, and it will appear between the covers, let the toes hurt that it tramps on. Here, with book publishers, stands the great redoubt of freedom of the press.

Before his typewriter had cooled from its long go-round with *The Big Sky*, Guthrie already had envisioned his next novel: He would enlarge on the westering theme he had introduced. He would rescue Dick Summers from the tedium of a Missouri farm and point him west again—this time at the head of a large and varied crew of new characters traveling the Oregon Trail during the summer of 1845.

Guthrie's publisher, William Sloane, was short on big titles, and so was pressing his star author hard for another book. In answer, Guthrie secluded himself, set to work and, in what he has described as "six months of such effort as I'll never be able to muster again," sculpted *The Way West*.

In drawing comparisons between *The Way West* and *The Big Sky*, biographer Charles Hood again quotes from *The English Journal* and Dayton Kohler's 1951 review, "A. B. Guthrie, Jr. and the West": "In *The Big Sky*," Kohler says, "Guthrie's fable is one of man outside society, but in *The Way West* his subject is society itself."

The Way West, like *The Big Sky*, furthers the premise of human transmogrification of the natural environment. But the earlier novel focuses on the negative—the dying-out of the grand and free social order of fur hunters and Plains Indians, while *The Way West* examines the other side of that same coin—the enthusiasm and high spirits of bold people forging a new order. Where the characters of *The Big Sky* look increasingly back as the novel progresses, those of *The Way West*—with the exception of Dick Summers—have their minds, hearts and eyes locked firmly forward, toward the setting sun and the promise they hail as Oregon. New land. Room to breathe.

This pioneers' dream is established in the opening paragraphs of *The Way West*. In conversation with his wife, Rebecca, protagonist Lije Evans lays out his feelings.

> "Oregon," he said, letting his thoughts drift, "it would be a good thing to a man, knowin' he had helped settle the country and so joined it to America."

Later, in answer to prodding from neighbor Dick Summers, Evans digs deeper into his motives for wanting to sell his Missouri farm and head for the West Coast.

"Why you goin', Lije? You didn't leave nothin' there."

"I told you. We got to take Oregon, Dick. I feel I got to help."

"That ain't all."

"No. I ain't been there, but I been here. I ain't satisfied just to work to keep myself up so's I can work some more. There ought to be more to livin' than that."

Good old Dick Summers (whom Guthrie acknowledges as his all-time favorite character and, to some extent, alter ego) at length gives in to the pleas of Evans and his fellow travelers, agreeing to guide their wagon train across the land he'd known so intimately in younger years. By recruiting Summers as pilot, Guthrie provides not just a bridge in viewpoint between past and present, but a powerful force of conscience to mellow the often-fierce expansionist drives of men new to the West and eager to bring the land and its inhabitants under their control. One such character is Mack. Early in the trip, he and Summers share an illustrative verbal exchange.

"Expecting trouble?" Mack asked.

"Maybe not. Those pore Kaws, though, they get hungry and cold. And stealin's fun to an Injun."

Mack said, "Damn nuisances," and felt a little surprise when Summers answered, "They got their ways, like we got ours. I reckon we're a heap big nuisance to them."

"I can't see it," Mack answered, though he did. He put an edge in his tone. "They'll have to learn."

He waited, but Summers answered only, "Reckon so."

Charles Hood has observed that "Guthrie's sadness over the plight of the Indian is expressed poignantly in his observations at an Indian graveyard he and [Randall] Swanberg visited near Lander, Wyoming," then goes on to quote from "Adventure with History," an article Guthrie penned for the July 14, 1953, number of *Holiday* magazine.

One grave had inscribed on it: "Buried like a white man." We looked at it quite a while. But for his white brother this Shoshone would have been tied in a tree and left to birds and weather, but now he was underground and had dirt in his mouth and was proud of it. Proud to be buried like the men who had forced their way of life on him and done so many of his fellows in. Sometimes a man imagines he can hear the angels crying.

For Brownie Evans, teenage son of Lije and Rebecca, the idea and reality of westering evokes none of the patriotic gusto displayed by his father, none of Mack's desire to conquer and tame the new land and its inhabitants. Rather, the journey brings to Brownie feelings not unlike those expressed by Boone Caudill and Jim Deakins when they first laid eyes on the upper Missouri country—the Oregon of *their* dreams. Feelings not unlike those Dick Summers felt in his early days in the West but which now bring to him only sadness in their remembering. Feelings perhaps even not unlike those felt by a young Bud Guthrie while out hunting, fishing and roaming free in his Montana childhood. From the internal monologue of Brownie Evans:

> He wouldn't want to tell about how it was with him, not even about the way his chest filled sometimes when he came to a rise and looked over the country or how his heart turned just at the smell of camp smoke or the lonely voices of the wild geese that had nested along the river. He would know then that good things awaited him, great things that he couldn't put a word to or set out in thought.

But for Dick Summers—a man "at home with sadness"—the journey west with wagons holds no dreams, just a replay of memory and musing, every creaking turn of the iron-rimmed wheels revealing—and bringing about—yet more change. Summers's nostalgia reaches its greatest depths—and Guthrie's artful crafting of internal monologue its greatest heights—when the train makes a stopover at bustling Fort Laramie. Here is a place Summers had known long ago as old Fort William and, before that, as a wilderness river crossing, a favored camping spot of fur trappers and the warring parties of Plains Indians who would sometimes harass the whites there.

> There was danger still, from Pawness and Sioux and maybe Blackfeet farther on, but it struck him as different, as somehow piddling. A cornfield, even like the sorry patch by the fort, didn't belong with war whoops and scalping knives. It belonged with cabins and women and children playing safe in the sun. It belonged with the dull pleasures, with the fat belly and the dim eye of safety. . . .

There was no place in the world these days for a mountain man, and less and less of it all the time. A few years more and a man fool enough to trap like as not would stumble on to a picnic. The buffalo were thinning. . . . In not so long a time now people in the mountains would be living on hog meat, unknowing the flavor and strength of fleece fat and hump ribs. Unknowing, either, how keen an enemy the Rees and the Blackfeet were. He almost wished for the old Rees, for the old Blackfeet that the white man's pox had undone. They had given spirit to life; every day lived was a day won.

Thus we are reminded in *The Way West*, via Summers's dismal comparisons of past to present to future, of the continual unfolding of the socio-environmental change forecast by Uncle Zeb Calloway in the early pages of *The Big Sky*.

And reminded, too, of the Indians' view of what the whites are calling progress. While palavering with a score of angry young Sioux who have taken Brownie Evans captive, Summers translates the words of their chief.

The Indians hearts were good. . . . The country belonged to them, but still they let the white brother pass. They let him kill meat and scare it away, so that they had to hunt far for it and their young ones cried hungry in their lodges.

Through this land of resentful Indians, beneath a sun "hot as a blister," the train creeps on, ever west. Seeing the determination and willing sacrifice of the pioneers, Summers recognizes that both the people and their motives are good—most of them, at least. But good or no, he can neither fully understand nor endorse the spirit of acquisition and growth and change and even patriotism that fills the well from which the pioneers draw their collective strength.

Strong folks, and strong for what? For Oregon and fish and farms, for wheat and sheep and nation. And now it came to him, while his own skull tapped to the heat, that that was what had ailed the mountain man—he didn't hanker after things: he had all that he wanted.

While Summers neither fully understands the motives nor totally endorses the actions of the pioneers, neither does he condemn them.

When Brother Weatherby, a Methodist missionary traveling with the train, comments on the grandness of the land they are moving across, Summers replies, "Looks just like it did," then lapses into a spell of internal monologue.

> While he answered, Summers thought it was only the earth that didn't change. It was just the mountains, watching others flower and seed, watching men come and go, the Indian first and after him the trapper, pushing up the unspoiled rivers, pleased with risk and loneliness, and now the wanters of new homes, the hunters of fortune, the would-be makers of a bigger nation, spelling the end to a time that was ended anyway.
>
> He didn't blame the Oregoners as he had known old mountain men to do. Everybody had his life to make, and every time its way, one different from another. The fur hunter didn't have title to the mountains no matter if he did say finders keepers. By that system the country belonged to the Indians, or maybe someone before them or someone before them. No use to stand against the stream of change and time.

And neither is A. B. Guthrie, Jr. attempting to stand against the stream of change and time when he points repeatedly in his writing to the environmental waste and destruction that too-rapid change, working insidiously behind the guises of progress and necessity, has left and continues to leave in its wake.

At novel's end, Dick Summers deposits his charges safe at their destination—a land already too tamed and populated for his liking—then disappears, without goodbyes, into the night. All we know of his plans are that he intends to work his way back to the Rockies, heading east to find the West, in hopes, we are left to assume, of piecing together something of a future amidst the landscape of his past.

Again from the Dayton Kohler review, as quoted in the Hood biography:

> Together, *The Big Sky* and *The Way West* sum up two periods of the history of a region.... It is clear that Guthrie is of two opinions about the frontier experience. As he projects it through the story of Lije Evans and the "On-to-Oregon" company, it is good, a promise of law and social stabilization in an area that has been solitary and wild. But in the closing chapter of *The Big Sky*

and in the musings of Dick Summers the reading is that the white man defiles nature through motives of greed and ruthless conquest.

Commenting on that interpretation, Hood adds:

Although Kohler correctly finds Guthrie to be of "two opinions" about the development of the West, he is wrong in assuming they are not compatible. Guthrie contends that one can accept civilization's expansion while disliking some of its consequences. He asks: "Don't we all have that dichotomy? As I get older, I dislike more and more what goes in the name of progress. I dislike crowds and I hate to see our wilderness disappear—very, very much. If that's a dichotomy, then I'm a victim of it."

A few weeks after delivering the manuscript for *The Way West* to his publisher, Guthrie traveled to the University of Montana to lecture at a conference on creative writing. While there, he received a telegram notifying him that his latest novel had made the Book of the Month Club for October 1949—no small literary honor bearing promise of no small monetary reward.

Months later, back in Lexington, Guthrie would receive a second telegram—this one informing him that he'd been awarded the 1950 Pulitzer Prize for Distinguished Fiction. The telegram, he noted, was signed by the president of Columbia University, one Dwight D. Eisenhower.

Seven years would pass before A. B. Guthrie, Jr. would publish the third novel in his evolving saga of the changing West. During this hiatus he would visit Hollywood to write the screenplay for the classic Alan Ladd movie, *Shane*, which earned him an Academy Award nomination for best screenplay. And he would undertake an adventure that would add yet another chapter to his knowledge and understanding of man's myopic manipulation of nature.

In 1950, Guthrie and his good friend Bernard ("Benny") DeVoto—the widely respected historian, iconoclast and author of *Across the Wide Missouri* whom Guthrie had first met in his Nieman days at Harvard—would travel the length of the Missouri River, from its headwaters in western Montana more than 2,500 miles downstream to its confluence with the Mississippi.

The trip was arranged by a mutual friend from the Bread Loaf days, Navy Commander Bill Lederer (the author of *The Ugly American*), who enlisted the U. S. Air Force and the Army Corps of Engineers as hosts and chauffeurs. Prior to the trip, Guthrie had held "an unstudied respect for the Corps." DeVoto, however, was acutely critical of the bulging bureaucracy's eager-beaver river-damming practices—a criticism which, during the course of the Missouri River journey, Guthrie would come to share and even expand upon.

In a converted Air Force B-25 bomber, the party droned over the Oregon Trail, ticking off its familiar landmarks—Scott's Bluff, Independence Rock, the Sweetwater River. They made two fly-overs of South Pass—an east-west gap in the north-south chain of the Rockies flanked by the rugged Rattlesnake and Wind River ranges, populated by both the spirits of Guthrie's fictional characters and the ghosts of their flesh-and-blood counterparts. Then the bomber steered north over the hoary peaks of the Bighorns and Absarokas and on to Great Falls.

At Great Falls the Air Force bomber and its crew were relieved by a Corps of Engineers DC-3 and crew, which flew the party to Three Forks, Montana—that geographic and historic landmark where the Jefferson, Gallatin and Madison rivers join their flows to form the headwaters of the Missouri.

From there the lumbering twin-engine transport carried Guthrie and DeVoto downriver, flying over one historic landmark after another: The Great Falls of the Missouri. Fort Benton, which in the mid-1800s had served as the upstream terminus of navigation on the Missouri. The site of long-gone Fort MacKenzie.

At Fort Peck, where the mighty river is plugged by a great dam, the two writers met with top Corps of Engineers brass—Generals Pick, Brown and Sturgis (men of a type, Guthrie would later write, who "can't endure the sight of running water"). They argued strenuously against the very dams the generals were building.

Later, to prove they held no animosity toward their generous hosts, the writers prevailed upon the generals for the loan of a small boat in order to float, rather than fly, a long stretch of the Missouri below Fort Peck Dam.

In his autobiography, Guthrie recalls the exuberance he and DeVoto felt while navigating the big river in a small, outboard-powered craft.

Just as of old. Just as if the old were now. And Benny and I were Lewis and Clark, seeing as they saw, running aground as they did, getting sunburned and calloused and developing that look of wonder that stares at you from old reports.

The voyagers floated on past the mouth of the Platte, then, using a combination of water, land and air transportation, followed the Missouri on to its juncture with the Mississippi north of St. Louis.

By 1953, Guthrie had been more than a quarter-century away from the place he still considered his "fix on the universe"—Montana's Teton River country. Over the years he had come to appreciate Kentucky and had grown to love many of its people and refined ways. But in the life of A. B. Guthrie, Jr., East would never preempt West. From his autobiography:

> The Bluegrass landscape did not enchant me, though I was informed that it should. White paneled fences, manicured fields, gentle rolls of land, orderly trees—these smacked too much of man. They were artificial and ephemeral. I told myself, thinking of Montana, that I liked my beauty grim. I liked it out of control, pristine, everlasting as man's work could never be.

And so it was, for the second time in his life, that Guthrie himself went westering, settling this time in Great Falls—less than 50 eagle-flight miles south and east of Choteau. He would visit his hometown frequently in the coming years, holing up when there on 800 acres of jackpine real estate he had purchased several years before as a family vacation retreat. The rocky land was dotted with two small lakes, two small cabins, and watched over by Ear Mountain rising four miles to the south and west. Local folk called the spread Twin Lakes. (Some years later, Guthrie would divide between the Nature Conservancy and his daughter, Helen, all but the 160 acres on which he and Carol now live.)

Home at last, Guthrie went to work on *These Thousand Hills*. Set in a rapidly changing Montana of the late 1800s, it's a thoughtful novel of broncs and their busters, wolves and their skinners, cattle and their punchers, and good times and hard. But in jumping from the pioneers of *The Way West* to the cattlemen of *These Thousand Hills*, Guthrie left a chronological gap spanning the 35 years from 1845 to 1880. This chink would not be filled until 1982 and the publication of *Fair Land, Fair Land*—

the last-written of Guthrie's six-novel saga of the West.

Thus, to maintain continuity in our tracing of socio-environmental themes through Guthrie's fiction, we'll take up *Fair Land, Fair Land* next, trailing that tireless tracker of the wilderness West, Dick Summers, from the shaded and sodden forests of coastal Oregon back across the prairies and mountains to the bright open skies of Montana.

FAIR LAND,
FAIR LAND

A.B. Guthrie, Jr. had been 81 years in the world when *Fair Land, Fair Land* was published by Houghton Mifflin in 1982. To paraphrase the author, while age may not make a man wise, eight decades of observing, comparing and assessing do give him certain advantages. At the least, we are left to hope, accruing years should bring us closer to sorting out our priorities, to finding the ground on which to make our stand—if a stand we are cut out to make.

In *Fair Land, Fair Land*, Guthrie demonstrates that indeed he has determined his priorities, taken his philosophical high ground and thereupon is standing firm. Here Guthrie is more direct and less allusive in presenting his *Weltanschauung* in general and his socio-environmental convictions in particular than in any of his other five novels of the protean West.

Given a single hint in *The Big Sky* and another in *Fair Land, Fair Land*, we know Dick Summers to be in his late 40s when *The Way West* closes in late 1845. Notwithstanding his painful nostalgia for a youth and a wilderness West that are all but gone, Summers has determined that his future must lie in parallel with his past. He reflects:

Mountains lasted and what else? The sky. The stars. Maybe the high plains and the riffling grasses, though like as not men would find a use for the land and gouge it up so's to raise turnips and cabbages or some other truck not worth eating. Before that was done, he aimed to have a long, good look again.

Tagging along with Summers for his "long, good look" at the end of an era is Higgins, a likable character introduced but left largely undeveloped in *The Way West*. Higgins is a physical scarecrow of a man with keen sensibilities and a kind heart.

While camped one night on their journey from Oregon to Montana, Higgins fires questions at Summers in an effort to map him out. Through Summers's replies, Guthrie summarizes critical aspects of the old trapper's personal history and philosophies for readers unfamiliar with the earlier novels. At the same time, the author restates the premise he established in *The Big Sky* and furthered in *The Way West*—that, generation after generation, men tend to destroy the things they cherish.

[Higgins] stirred the pot with a stick. "I got it in my head you're fightin' shy of people. Ain't it so?"

"For now, anyhow."

"You got somethin' against 'em?"

"Just get tired of 'em in time. They spoil things."

"Like what?"

"Like ways of living.' Look. The Indians had fixed things pretty nice. They killed just what they had to. They didn't count up what they had unless it was stole horses. . . . They didn't have any idea of markin' off a piece of ground and sayin', 'This is mine.' The land belonged to all of 'em. . . . Then along came the white man. He wanted furs. He wanted land. And for trade he brought along whiskey or what passed for it."

"I guess you couldn't blame him, except for the firewater."

The pot was beginning to boil.

"It's a way of things, and I was some part of it, trappin' beavers, findin' trails for others to follow, havin' one hell of a time without thinkin'. . . ."

They fell silent. Summers was just as glad to let the matter lie there. He wasn't good at explaining things, even to himself, he thought. It was the goodbyes that ate at him, the goodbyes to what was, the coming goodbyes to even what now was. . . .

"And that's why we're goin' where we're goin'?"

"One reason. To see what's left. To pleasure ourselves while we can."

A star fell down the sky, and the breeze stirred the ash of the fire, and Summers said for good-night while he looked up, "More damn people than all the stars."

In *Fair Land, Fair Land* a new but related concern confronts Summers, a concern reflective of events in Guthrie's life at the time—the plight of the grizzly bear.

Trailing along the upper Big Blackfoot River near the Continental Divide, Summers and Higgins come upon the unconscious hulk of a gigantic gunshot-wounded grizzly.

Higgins sucked in his breath as they rounded the turn. He wheezed out, "God! Good God!"

"Lost a foreleg above the second joint. . . ."

"You goin' to put him out of his misery?"

Summers got down on one knee, resting his Hawken on the other. "Ephraim, Old Ephraim," he said.

"How's that?"

"I call to mind—" He didn't go on. He called to mind old days with the beaver traps, and young men, the traps lifted, sitting around campfires, and they would speak of Old Ephraim, the great white bear, and their tones held respect and awe and a sort of love, as if Ephraim somehow was a part of them, a living marker of the wild life they lived. Old Ephraim. . . .

"It ain't right. Why don't they leave him alone?"

"I never heard you take on over a critter, and him nigh onto dead."

"It's not just the one I'm thinkin' on. It's the whole breed, the whole goddam family. What can you say later on? 'Yep, there was grizzlies in them days? There was Ephraim. You should have seen him.' "

After placing a bucket of water and some deer meat within reach of the bear, the men backtrail a safe distance and make camp. The following morning both the bear and the offerings left for it are gone. As the partners ride on, Summers suspects the creature of following them and so puts out more food to aid its recovery and encourage its trust.

On the east side of the Divide the pair meet a rider headed the other way. The man's name is Brewer, and he asks if they've seen a bear or a blood trail.

> "It was like this," Brewer said. "I was huntin' buffalo, two or three days down the line, and I seen this here monster and fired. Hit him, too. He made off into the bushes with a foreleg floppin'. . . ."
> "So you aim to finish him off?"
> "Course."
> "Why?"
> "So I can say I kilt him, the biggest grizzly any man ever seen."

To put this early day trophy hunter off, Summers and Higgins deny seeing the bear or sign of him and concoct an impromptu story about having narrowly escaped a Blackfeet war party back down the trail a ways. Brewer breaks off his hunt and retreats.

The premise of this scene and related scenes following—that the grizzly bear is the grandest living symbol of wilderness America and so should be respected and protected—has been a major theme in Guthrie's conservation efforts throughout the 1980s.

Time flows on, years of it, with Summers and Higgins more or less settled in the valley of the Teton River, their tepees pitched close below a mountain looking something like an ear turned on its side. Enter Brother Potter, a cheerful frontier missionary whose exuberant gratitude to his God leads Hig into a bout of anti-anthropocentric sentiment reminiscent of the soul-searching of Jim Deakins in *The Big Sky*. Potter is speaking:

> "Look about you. Everywhere is plenty. The beasts of the fields, the birds of the air, all put there for man, for his food or his delight. Look at the soil that grows food for us. Look at the skies that give us sunshine and rain. It is all God's bounty, his gifts to mankind. . . ."
> Higgins smoked for a while longer. So everything was made for man, was it? Seemed like the other critters ought to have a vote in the final say. They were here, and along comes Mr. High and Mighty Man and says you're all mine. You were made just for me. Talk about being meek.

Time passes, change approaches.

The past spring had seen a big party of whites, though—men, wagons, teams and tackle—and some men sighted through instruments and others held poles, and once in a while they planted a stake, and Summers knew them for surveyors. It was Blackfoot country, this country was, made so by treaty, but here was the advance party of whites getting ready to parcel it out.

To combat this foreboding incursion of civilization upon their wilderness redoubt, Summers and Hig employ a tactic that, in the twentieth century, would come (thanks to writer Edward Abbey) to be known as "monkey-wrenching," or sabotage intended to protect the environment.

[The surveyors] had gone on, leaving no signs of their passage except for a here-and-there marker, which Summers and Higgins tore from the ground when they came on them.

By and by, rumors reach the partners of a gold strike at Alder Gulch. Disturbed and curious, they ride out to investigate. At the boomtown that has sprung up along the gulch they come face-to-face with the raw edge of too-rapid change.

A good part of the camp was tents, staked to the ground or to wood platforms. Some places were part tent and part wood. The best were built of poles or logs or whipsawed lumber, and a man could throw a cat through the cracks. . . .
The smell of the place reached him before he came to it. This was what men did, what bunches of men did—tear up and stink up a location and foul the water and leave the land wrecked when the gold ran out, leave the land torn and the water nasty until maybe at last God got around to mending things. No guarantee that he would.

Toward the end of the novel, Summers, having seen a great deal of change in his 70-plus years, muses:

Everything was new as of its time. And everything was old, or would be with the years. Nothing stayed put. Men came with their big ideas, looking to a future that would laugh at their work.

Why not let things be? Why the hurry to play hell with what was? That was the way of man. That was the way of men who bred and increased and reached out.

Finally, with civilization crowding ever closer to the valley of the Teton, the partners decide to move on rather than remain to see the place that has been the center of their universe despoiled by so-called progress. In a poignant gesture of gratitude to the land that has fed and clothed and meant so much to the old mountain man for so very long, Summers fires his little cabin on the Teton. Watching his home burn and his personal history there dissipate with the smoke, he observes:

"Best to leave it as we found it. That's what I'm thinkin'. New-like but old."

When, after a run of three novels, Dick Summers finally exits, it is in a scene and under circumstances both appropriate to and symbolic of the socio-environmental themes Guthrie used him to express throughout a long and compelling fictional career.

THESE

THOUSAND

HILLS

With the publication of *These Thousand Hills* (Houghton Mifflin, 1956), A. B. Guthrie, Jr. was at the midpoint in his emerging six-novel saga of the peopling of the West. The book forwarded the chronology of his series to within little more than a decade of his own birth. He was now writing of an era recent enough to allow him to draw on not just recorded, but living history. In his prefatory note to the novel he says:

> No man of our day can write about the West of the 1880's without reading about it. If he is very lucky, as I have been, he may remember vestiges of that vanished period and he may have friends among the few aged old-timers who will help fill him in.

In the final chapter of *The Blue Hen's Chick*, written in 1964, Guthrie describes *These Thousand Hills* as his "most difficult and least successful [novel] . . . because it dealt with the cowpuncher and had to avoid, if it could, the stylized Western myth."

This struggle for historic realism forced Guthrie to keep the story necked tight to characterization and action, with the result that the players in *These Thousand Hills* have less room to reflect on social and environmental questions than had Dick Summers and others in *The Big Sky*, *The Way West* and *Fair Land, Fair Land*. Even so, *These Thousand Hills* is ripe with environmental comment.

In the space of the first two paragraphs of the novel, Guthrie not only introduces his young protagonist and reveals a great deal about the boy's character, history and hopes, but also smoothly recapitulates his cornerstone socio-environmental premise . . . that each generation tends to destroy the thing it cherishes, with always a new generation coming up to search out something new to love to death. The year is 1880, the place is Oregon.

> These three old men would sit and smoke and let a word fall and pause to hear the echoes of it as if they owned all time to speak their little pieces in.
>
> Lat Evans shifted his seat on the ground, finding patience in the thought that their talk didn't matter now, and looked off to where dusk was putting a dull shine on the river. It was good and lonely water once, the Umatilla was, before people had begun coming in to spoil it, bringing plows to rip up pastures and cattle to graze ranges already overgrazed and sheep to make affairs still worse. That was the trouble with all Oregon, here and elsewhere even more—too many people, too much stock, too many homestead claims, and so wildlife was disappearing and cows were poor in flesh and price, and streams ran tame and clouded . . . .

To get away, Evans signs on with a cattle drive bound for Montana Territory. Arriving there in the fall, he and three fellow drovers decide to spend the winter wolfing. While blizzard-bound in a tumble-down cabin, one of the group—an old-timer named Godwin—falls to reminiscing about how radically and rapidly the country roundabouts has changed. In describing how buffalo numbered beyond counting no more than a dozen years before and since have all but disappeared, Godwin calls on anecdote. Back in 1867, having canoed down the Missouri to a place called Cow Island, Godwin and his companions came upon the steamboat *Imperial* afloat in a river of bison.

> "So we paddled down, and there, close to the mouth of the

Yellowstone, they was makin' a crossin' — more buffalo than a man could count in all the time since old Adam, more'n there's a name for or a spyglass built strong enough to find the lead and drag of. The pilot he banged right into the middle of 'em and backed up the paddles so as to stay there, and everyone run to the rails and began blazin' away, with rifles and fusees and scatterguns and pistols and pea-shooters and whatever threw lead. Three hundred dead-game sports there was, allow a few one way or the other, all havin' the time of their lives while the buffalo swam crazy and wore themselves out, a big bunch just drowndin' and a bunch gettin' bullet-killed and the wounded and weak boggin' down in the shore mud and waitin' there helpless while a hell's slew of wolves danced on the bank . . . .

"Big doin's. A whole damn world full of God's best eatin', and we kill it off so's to make room for them sea-lion, swamp-angel, bull-tough, piss-poor cattle from Texas."

When one of Godwin's listeners indicates that perhaps the storyteller doesn't have so much room to be critical, considering that "you're still killin' " buffalo, Godwin see's his critic's point and replies:

"Yeah, for grub and for baits, and one gun don't make any difference much." The force had gone out of Godwin's voice. "It's the order of things, the teetotal end of the buffalo is, and where's the man that can change it?"

With the buffalo thinned out, wolves too are proving hard to find along the Musselshell River where the four men have been putting out poisoned baits. Thus, when the weather breaks they move on, traveling slowly across the empty winter landscape until finally sighting a remnant herd of bison.

A long way off a herd crested a hill and began to pour down it, and Godwin pointed that way. "Take a good look, boys, at them and the others. Take a good look so's you can tell your children."

But just as Lije Evans, in *The Way West*, had dreamed of a big new life in what to him was an untarnished wilderness while old-timer Dick Summers's thoughts ran to nostalgia, so does Lije's grandson, Lat, disregard the remembrances of old Godwin and dream of his own future in a land new to him.

So much of prairie, of miles endless and vacant, allowed chances and choices beyond all reasonable hope. It did now, at this minute, as Oregon must have before crowds wore the trail to it deep. All that was needed was cattle or money for cattle. That was all.

Lat Evans in due time realizes his dreams. And, as did those who had come west and passed on before him, he cherishes the land as if it had been designed and made especially for him, with all time and events past adding up to no more than preparation for the now. But Evans is to witness one last ghostly reminder of a time only just passing to memory.

Farther on, with night closing down, he spotted a blotch on the hazed sheet of the earth and reined in to look. The blotch moved, setting in movement smaller blotches around it. He kicked the Appaloosie.

Wolves and a stray cow, or a bull, three wolves circling round, dashing in and back out. The stray wheeled to meet them. Lat blinked and looked again.

He had come out of nowhere, this ancient buffalo bull, out of hidden hills or lost plains or the great hole in the ground that the Indians invented to account for the disappearance of the herds they once knew. A lone bull, the last bull, looking at the places the wolves had just left. . . .

The bull didn't move except to front the new danger. Starved to bones, rimed with frost, he stood with his head down, daring anyone to come on, daring the world and everything in it. Above his stubborn eyes his forelock dangled, still fuzzed with last season's burrs, still sandy from remembered wallows, from watering places he wouldn't see any more. The blizzard had driven him, the wind and the cutting snow, out of some echoing solitude down here to ranges made strange since he grazed as a calf. . . .

There was nothing to do but ride on.

In 1960, Houghton Mifflin released *The Big It*, a collection of 13 of Guthrie's short stories, including the powerful mountain-man tales "Last Snake" and "Mountain Medicine." Of the collection, Oliver La Farge, writing for *The New York Times*, said, "Compared to the stylized claptrap of screen and T.V., *The Big It* is like a Frontier Model Colt .45 alongside a collection of cap pistols."

In 1962, Bud and Harriet Guthrie were divorced. Guthrie continued to write, temporarily switching from fiction to nonfiction, producing the autobiographical *The Blue Hen's Chick: A Life in Context* in 1965. The 261 pages of this compelling and unpretentious book reveal the Pulitzer-winning writer to be a modest man with wide-ranging interests and concerns. And here, too, the reader is given a scattered but intensely personal look at the development and expression of Guthrie's environmental philosophies, beginning with his Choteau childhood and extending through the middle of his sixth decade.

In 1967, Guthrie met Carol Bischman Luthin, an attractive and intelligent woman many years younger than he. In 1969, they were married. He says of her, "She's the best critic I've encountered in a long lifetime," and "She's a wonderful woman. Marrying me is the only cause I've had to doubt her sanity."

Now Guthrie returned to his old Corona with new vigor. His next project would follow the autobiographical lead of *The Blue Hen's Chick* by reinterpreting the country and characters of his Choteau childhood in semi-autobiographical fiction. Released by Houghton Mifflin in 1970, *Arfive* brought Guthrie's West into the twentieth century.

ARFIVE

A. B. Guthrie, Jr.'s fiction never strays far from historical fact. Thus, by the opening of the twentieth century, the era treated in *Arfive*, he has narrowed his focus to parallel the narrowing West, concentrating on one small Montana community. That community is Arfive, and it is modeled after Guthrie's hometown of Choteau. Here those two familiar Guthrie-country landmarks—the Teton River and Ear Mountain—are referred to as the Breast River and Elephant Ear Butte.

In existence no more than a score of years, Arfive is growing slowly from frontier outpost to settled community. In the book's opening pages, in a scene of foreshadowing presented by a minor but far-seeing character, Mr. McLaine, Guthrie provides a glimpse of events to come.

"It is in the nature of things as camps grow older. First, lawlessness, then loose law and order, then churches and schools and social sanctions and, finally, a town, not a camp. The preacher

41

and the schoolmaster are harbingers, and homesteaders will hasten the change."

The schoolmaster whom McLaine refers to is "Professor" Benton Collingsworth, the novel's character of primary viewpoint and a personality modeled after Guthrie's father. Like the senior Guthrie, "Prof" Collingsworth is an eastern-college educated, free-thinking man whose world view emanates from a curious and sometimes combative combination of Methodist fundamentalism and Thoreauvian naturalism.

Shortly after his arrival in Arfive to become principal of the area's first high school, Collingsworth takes fly rod in hand and hikes the short distance from town to the limpid Breast River. While fishing, he reflects on the West—its past, present and the role he would play in the making of its future.

A V'd riffle troubled the water, its dark point moving with purpose; and now he could see the legs working and the flat tail idle in tow. A beaver, his first one, unmistakable. He breathed softly, not moving until the pistol spank of the tail startled him. Left to see was only a wash in the pond, a riffled memory of what might have been. . . .

He saw himself in another time, looking for beaver sign and setting his traps and in his hunt giving names to strange streams and finding passes that later generations would travel. But for beaver he might not be here himself. He saluted the dying riffle, glad that one of his creditors lived.

If that former time was good, this time was good enough, this time and this place. That poor, often-right, sometimes-eloquent New Englander, Thoreau, whose aim was a life with wide margins and whose feet, left to themselves, always pointed him west but didn't carry him far. Here were his margins. Here was his west.

But the fresh, wide-margined West seen by Collingsworth is to other eyes tired and atrophied. On another outing, the Professor crosses paths with an aging frontiersman named Charlie Blackman. Collingsworth asks him about old times along the Breast.

Charlie spit and looked into distance, and the shimmer of remembrance shown in his eyes. "I can call to mind," he said, and let his subject trail off.

"Yes?"

"Course, I wasn't around when doin's was real high, not for beaver. But buffalo, man alive, and wolfin' along with it. I seen anyhow a thousand head centered here where we're standin' and wolves taggin' the cripples. Man alive. . . . Ain't anything like it used to be."

"I suppose not, but cheer up, Charlie. This is still a young land."

Charlie's remembering eyes came to focus in what might have been pity. "Young? To you, I'm thinkin'. Whatever is old to the young? Tell me that. Nothin', that's what, except old men like yours truly."

A young country grown old through aging vision, Collingsworth reflected as he walked on. The eye of the beholder. But not entirely. Things had changed since Charlie's youth and would change still more, not the mountains, not the sky, but the earth and the habits of men. . . .

Here, as schoolteacher and even as churchman, he felt a touch of discomfort, for he was part, as well as agent, of change. To his inner ear came the words of old Mr. McLaine.

"Change is the order of nature," he had said. His beard swung to the shake of his head. "It is our nature somehow to resist while forwarding it. What comes comes, to our dismay or delight or more likely both, and both diminished."

A second *Arfive* character of significant viewpoint is a sturdy rancher named Mort Ewing. In contrast to the refined newcomer Collingsworth, Ewing has been long in the West and is decidedly rough-hewn. For him, the future is arriving far too suddenly.

From a height the town of Arfive came to sight. Men would be drinking there, breathing air that their crowded breath and their tobacco and bodies had fouled. Or they would be talking prices and prospects and portents of winter. Or investments and interest and what they called progress.

By recognizing and counting, each from his own prospect, the losses as well as the gains attendant to change, Ewing and Collingsworth remain intellectually distanced from what is being called progress even though, as rancher and teacher, they are cogs in its insidious mechanism.

The harbingers of change in *The Big Sky* were the Oregon pioneers; in *Fair Land, Fair Land* they were miners and soldiers and cattlemen; now, in *Arfive*, they are dry-land homesteaders. At first merely bemused by the flood of immigrant farmers taking up hopeless postage-stamp homesteads around Arfive, the Professor soon becomes openly doubtful.

Collingsworth pulled on his pipe and looked down and afar to the far-scattered patches of land torn by the plow, to the farm sites staked out by the hopeful. . . .

Here and there he saw a few buildings, the make-do and alien shelters and outhouses of homesteaders and the turned-over fields lying stark. And he had now to think of them as impertinences, as violations of the first and true purpose, no matter the Christian ethic that the earth was created for man. Man would put it to his use, never fear. Let fellow creatures go hang. The land was there to tear up, as elsewhere were forests to fell and minerals to gouge out and streams to force out of true for wheels, pastures and crops. Leave it to man. Leave man to what was his. To the devil, then, with men like that heretical former president, Theodore Roosevelt, and his colleague Gifford Pinchot, who had acted to conserve the forests of the public domain.

Collingsworth is joined in his resentment of the "impertinences" of the immigrant farmers by a perceptive half-breed named Smoky Moreau. Afield one day with Collingsworth, Moreau offers a red man's view of this white man's use of the land called homesteading.

There was brooding in the dark eyes. He turned them then to the valley and plains, and his arm made a sweep. "Man, he is not so much as he thinks. Not by-damn homesteaders for sure. They say 'mine' for land not their own. They turn over the good grass. They plant seed this earth does not know. But no medicine big enough. Snow, cold, no rain. They will freeze up and dry up and go, those homesteaders."

It was seldom Smoky spoke at such length. Collingsworth answered, "They have been told that rain follows the plow."

Smoky spat. "Weeds follow. Dust. They make desert."

"We'll have to see."

And see they would.

In the opening page of *Arfive*, as Mort Ewing drove the Collingsworth family by stage from a remote train depot to Arfive, the Professor spotted a fleeing herd of pronghorn antelope, prompting Ewing to comment on their abundance and "good eating" virtues. In a subtle irony at novel's end, one of Ewing's final statements reflects back on that scene. Driving with his wife—horses and coach supplanted by an early model automobile, Ewing observes:

> "Don't see any antelopes along the road anymore.... Nor anywhere else. The homesteaders poached 'em. Had to or croak."

In 1970, the year of its publication, *Arfive* won for its author the prestigious Western Heritage Award.

The following year, the editors of *The Sunday Missoulian* asked Guthrie to pen an introduction to that paper's special coverage of Earth Week, 1971. The enthusiastic response to that brief but poignant essay (titled "A Message to the Young" in Part II) launched Guthrie on a series of public appearances in behalf of conserving what remained unspoiled in the West—a campaign that would see the composition and delivery of a dozen compelling speeches in as many years.

In 1972, Guthrie's fiction again was honored, this time earning the Western Literature Association's Distinguished Achievement Award.

The following year, for a change of pace, Guthrie interrupted his series of historical novels (two more were yet to come) to produce a "fun" book. *Wild Pitch* (Houghton Mifflin, 1973) was the first in what eventually would grow into a series of four novels (a fifth is in the works at this writing) that Guthrie refers to as "Western whodunits." Although not of a type with *The Big Sky* and its brethren, these novels nonetheless provide excellent reading; they are entertaining, tightly crafted works of contemporary mystery set in the rural West. And neither do they lack of socio-environmental comment.

A busy 1973 also saw the publication of *Once Upon A Pond*, a collection of stories for children that Guthrie had been telling for the entertainment of little people for some 40 years.

Returning again to literature, the tireless writer began crafting a novel that, at the time of its publication by Houghton Mifflin in 1975, he announced as the conclusion of his historical saga. The title he chose for the book is appropriate to that intention: *The Last Valley*.

THE

LAST

VALLEY

From *The Big Sky* to *The Last Valley* we go from a macroview of untrammeled wilderness to a microview of the Teton River valley. The area serves as the vital connection between men and land in all but one of Guthrie's six novels of the maturing West.

The Last Valley is a sequel to *Arfive*, continuing the lives of Benton Collingsworth and Mort Ewing and their families and friends living in and around Arfive. But the protagonist of *The Last Valley* is a new character, a newspaperman named Ben Tate who turns up in Arfive at age 28, a few years after the end of World War I.

Ewing and Collingsworth soon befriend young Tate, who has purchased Arfive's weekly newspaper. The Professor offers counsel:

> "If I dare to give one bit of advice, Mr. Tate, it is this: be chary that you don't assume the coloration of the community."
>
> "The community isn't bad?"
>
> "Oh, no. Only provincial, only parochial, as are other com-

munities, little or big, in their way. . . ."

"My chunk of advice ain't so weighty," Ewing said. "It's just watch out for progress because you can't backtrack."

With youthful exuberance—and in part because he sees it as the responsibility of a newspaperman to his community—Ben Tate becomes an economic booster and champion of progress. Still, he isn't blind to careless change or hesitant to speak out against it in print or allow others do so.

The piece . . . had been prompted by the news that a federal hunter had been hired to put an end to the coyotes that roamed near the Breast River, a few miles north and west of the town. He had titled it "Coyote Song or Lamb Blat?" It was a sort of hymn to wilderness, to loneliness and the cry that came from it, and it included the point, in expert, accented prose, that sheep kill-ings, blamed on coyotes, were as often or oftener than not the work of town and ranch dogs. The detection of a guilty dog two days after the paper came out had modified criticism.

The author of that editorial was not Ben Tate, but Mary Jess Coll-ingsworth, daughter of the Professor. Mary Jess possesses an acute awareness of history, of the diverse values of wilderness and the impor-tance of conserving nature. This awareness is highlighted in conversa-tion with Tate at a scenic overlook near town.

After a silence she said, her eyes lost in looking, "Look, Ben. Just look."

He could see the canyon of the Breast River, purple with distance, and the meandering, tree-fringed flow of the stream, and the buttes and foothills that separated mountains and river, and it seemed to him that all bore the unchanging face of forever. . . .

"There would be tepees in the big bend of the river," she went on, "and smoke rising straight from the smokeholes and the horse herd nearby and buffalo on the ridge to the south. And no one would foreclose or compel others to sell what little they had. . . ."

"But no telephones, though," he said to break his own spell. "No electric lights or power. No radios. No automobiles."

"But no ugly fences, no torn earth and no buying and selling and counting the cost of profit."

By and by, in the name of flood control, irrigation, jobs, community welfare and, always, progress, the river that ribbons through that beautiful valley is dammed, the valley itself destined to be flooded.

At this point we are introduced to a new character with a new point of view. Jasper "Jap" York is a crusty old hunting guide and outfitter who has long enjoyed an intimate relationship with the backcountry, in particular the valley a large portion of which is about to be inundated by the dam. In streamside conversation with Ben Tate, York lays out his feelings.

"How are you, Jap?"

"The happy loafer on horseback, that's me. Horse is grazin' over yonder. But how am I for a fact?" The rumble of blasting came from downstream, and Ben could feel a quiver of earth. "I'm thinkin' the Bible played hell when it said the earth was made for man. That's how I am."

York got out a pipe, crumbled tobacco in his palm and lit up. The stream talked, and a breath of breeze played with a leaf. "Make the most of it while you can," York said. His eyes rose to the mountain side and lifted to the clear sky.

"This here," York went on, waving his pipe stem. "This grass, them trees, them posies along the bank, brutes, big and little, the mountains theirselves." His head moved in a slow shake. "That Jesus Christ dam!"

"You have to think of men."

"Men. Yeah, men. I had a pet onct, a cub bear, just the one, and I cared a heap for him. But bears by the bushel, bear after bear in bear country, why, I guide dudes to shoot 'em and don't cry a tear. If only one dandelion grew, you'd have to add to the grandstand."

Ben grinned, as he imagined York wanted him to. "But, Jap," he said, "you can't stand in the way of things. In your own lifetime you've seen a lot of changes."

"Can't call to mind any good ones right now."

In a subsequent scene, the anachronistic woodsman adds:

"A man in town," York said, "he just sees strangers walkin' the street and goddamn radios playin' what he don't want to hear, and everybody yappin' for progress, and the air foul with engine farts. Give me the good smell of horseshit. Let me hear a coyote."

Later, sheriff Frank Brobeck echoes York's sentiments.

"Say, Ben, you heart and soul, so to speak, for the dam? Hundred percent, I mean?"

"You ought to know. I've been plugging it long enough. . . ."

"But still the dam means sayin' so long, so long to the runs and holes we used to fish, so long to huntin' grounds and campin' grounds and pretty places we knew once."

"But if every change is goodbye to what was, it's hello to something new and something better. At least we can believe so. You've got me preaching now, but we can't say no to the future. If the first men in the West had said no, there'd be no Montana, no Arfive."

"Which, I guess, wouldn't have bothered them much. . . ."

When, some years later, Arfive suffers the worst flood in its history—made substantially worse by the dam on the Breast—Ben Tate finally recognizes and begins to acknowledge the unfortunate cumulative product of the change he has for so long boosted as necessary and beneficial.

"I had a sneaking hunch that goddamn dam never should have been built in the first place," Brobeck said after turning the truck around. "Flood control, they called it."

"Yep," Ewing answered. "You might say it's a washout, washed out or not."

"That's not the whole of it, not the sole reason," Ben said. Brobeck asked, "That so?"

"You have to allow for overgrazing and overcropping and timber up on the headwaters that never should have been cut. So, quick run-off. So, big water."

"Yes to all that," Ewing said. "At every turn, sometimes it seems to me, man fucks himself."

Guthrie takes advantage of the fact that the closing pages of *The Last Valley* are set in modern times—that is, the mid-1900s—to broach two contemporary socio-environmental concerns, touching first on the insidious threat to western agriculture from alkalinization caused by poorly managed irrigation and summer fallowing; then, via the internal monologue of Ben Tate, pondering the specter of nuclear holocaust.

The bomb. The atomic bomb, dropped on Japan perhaps with good reason. But a terror had been loosed nonetheless, and those who found a comfort in America's sole control of it surely were shortsighted or blind. What the nation could do, so could others in time. He could see the new generation, maybe many generations, living under the shadow of doom, until at last maybe the long fear would numb people. Could the young hope of life, the gay spirit, the confidence in the promise of being, could they continue under the hovering threat?

By novel's end, time and men have transmogrified the valley of the Breast, Guthrie's last valley. Most if not all of the changes carry with them regrets for what has been lost along the way—regrets even the once-progressive Ben Tate has come to feel.

> No longer did prairie chickens nest where they used to, within walking distance from Main Street. Their cover was gone, torn up and appropriated by homes and paving and gas stations, the last of the birds dropped by eager shotguns. No more could a man walk a mile or so west to the Breast and catch trout. The slowed and muddied stream held no more than suckers and chubs.

Guthrie reveals the full extent of Tate's belated conservation epiphany in a scene that serves not only as a denouement for *The Last Valley*, but as a forward-looking culmination of the socio-environmental themes introduced in *The Big Sky* and reiterated in subsequent novels. In conversation with Mike Murchison, a young World War II veteran planning a career in newspaper journalism—the very image of Ben himself a generation earlier—Tate expounds on what he has learned from the past and how he intends to apply that hard-won knowledge to the future.

> "Have you read Robert Frost?"
> "A little, I guess."
> "He wrote that the land was ours before we were the land's. A nice sentiment but not true as I see it. The land doesn't possess us. Hell, we abuse it every day so long as abuse brings a profit."
> "Yes, sir?"
> "We still have to learn to love and cherish and protect it. We're crazy. We can't keep digging and cutting and polluting. We

can't keep poisoning and exhausting our topsoil or giving it to the wind. We can't if we want to survive. . . . Just remember that the earth is all we have. Her riches are limited. When she goes, we go. That's plain to see, or should be. But in the name of progress we keep drawing on an account that can be overdrawn. Progress. Progress be damned! Progress leaves us no retreat. What is called progress doesn't."

"So, then?"

"So here's the positive. Here's a coming, great role of a good and free press. Here's what you can do and I can try to do as long as I last. . . . Educate. Inform. Look to the years ahead. Make people think. Speak from knowledge and concern for the future. That's not all you can do, but it's one hell of a challenge, and you'll have to fight." It struck Ben that he had been speaking with heat. He let the heat go. "If only we can get people to love the earth."

BUD

AND THE

BEARS

The following letter, written by A. B. Guthrie, Jr. in response to a petition being circulated by a handful of Front Range ranchers seeking to have the grizzly bear removed from the Endangered Species list, appeared in the November 14, 1985, edition of the *Choteau Acantha* (the same paper young Guthrie had worked for as after-school printer's devil).

Dear Editor:

Oh, come now, Mr. Ira Perkins, you with 224 signers to a petition that seeks to remove the grizzly bear from the Endangered Species list. Will you answer some questions and consider some rebuttals?

How many of your signers are stockmen who lease government land in grizzly bear habitat? Those people lease that land with full knowledge of the risks. How many signers with no real conviction signed just out of courtesy? How many tradespeople and commercial operators signed for fear of losing business if they didn't?

I am puzzled by your word "re-introduction" when you speak of the grizzly. Presumably the original introduction was made by God, or nature if you will. Accepting for the moment the wild and unsound assumption that human forces are re-introducing the grizzly, perhaps you, Mr. Perkins, as a God-fearing man, should praise them for continuing the Lord's work.

But this suggestion and your allegations of willful injury to ranchers' interests are nonsense. Who are these men you accuse? What interests and agencies are guilty? In fact, there are none, and none with the objectives you mention. None, Mr. Perkins. No man or outfit has transported bears to the Rocky Mountain Front, no matter how rumor has it. Instead, wildlife officials have removed problem bears to other regions, admittedly without too much success. Give them credit for trying. And your veiled slur on the Nature Conservancy is without basis in fact. Here, you are looking for a scapegoat. Make sure of your facts, man.

No, Mr. Perkins, you do not mean the re-introduction of the grizzly. You mean its reappearance out on the plains for the first time in the memory of the oldest inhabitant. Of that fact there can be no doubt.

But have you considered the reasons? Have you considered the careless disposal of dead livestock by ranchers, and, especially, feedlots? Feedlots are a rather recent entry on the Front. The coincidence of feedlots and the reappearance of the bears can not be overlooked.

There are not hundreds of bears in Idaho and Wyoming, as the petition suggests. There are a few. But the great majority of the animals, outside the parks and outside Canada and Alaska, reside in Montana. That is a fact that makes us almost unique among the 48 states. It brings tourists and other visitors, who spend money at motels, gas stations and stores. The very thought of seeing a grizzly, of being in bear country, is an enticement and a thrill. Have you included the businesses they patronize in your poll?

You describe the grizzly as horrendous and monstrous. Others have called it magnificent. Still others have said it was wilderness itself. And still others have said it was the grandest animal native to the country.

So come on, Mr. Perkins. Do you want to pasteurize Montana? Where is your pioneer spirit?

—A. B. Guthrie, Jr.

[Editor's note: In the spring of 1987, a suit filed by Ira Perkins and two other Front Range ranchers, contending that the Endangered Species Act was unconstitutional, was dismissed by the court.]

The fate of the grizzly has been a special concern for Guthrie throughout the 1980s. For that reason, both the history of the controversy surrounding the bear's presence along Montana's Rocky Mountain Front and Guthrie's role in that controversy deserve scrutiny here.

Choteau was founded as an agircultural community in the 1880s. Soon the surrounding area was settled by ranchers and farmers. By the turn of the century the grizzly bear, which historically had inhabited the fertile plains and prairies as far east as the Mississippi and its feeder streams, had been severely reduced in numbers, and the survivors driven into the western mountains. Even there, except in Montana, his numbers today are so small as hardly to be counted. This forced withdrawal was gradual, brought about not only by settlement but by the plow, deforestation, and hunters' guns.

Then, in the early 1980s, something or some combination of things began drawing a few bears down from the mountains onto the plains near Choteau, especially in the spring.

The bears' usual routes of travel from and back into the mountains are wooded and brushy stream corridors, in particular the Teton River and Willow Creek. A typical destination is the Nature Conservancy's 12,000-acre Pine Butte Swamp Preserve, an area rich in the green vegetation critical to the big omnivores' diets, especially just following a winter's hibernation. (A surprising statistic for those who envision the grizzly primarily as a predator: Up to 80 percent of the animal's diet is composed of graze; you are far more likely to see a wild grizzly eating wildflowers than devouring the carcass of some unfortunate prey animal.)

By and by, sheepmen in the area began reporting bear predation on their flocks. On rare occasion a beef cow was attacked or commercial beehives were pilfered. And people who sighted bears, on occasion literally at their doorsteps, were understandably frightened. Thus arose a clamor of resistance to the Front Range "grizzly threat," notwithstanding that no one had been killed or injured in a local bear attack within the memory of all but the most senior Choteau residents. Guthrie and others came promptly to the bears' defense, and the grizzly controversy was born.

Many of the grizzly's friends and potential defenders, it turned out, quickly grew shy of speaking their minds in public; after all, Choteau is a tiny town, the grizzly's foes in the area are loud and forceful, and few people welcome being ostracized in their own community.

While Guthrie doesn't enjoy incurring the rancor of his neighbors, neither does he shrink from it. He has proven to be far and away the most courageous and outspoken of the bear's supporters, hearing but not fearing the derision of the opposition.

In deference to the bear's less gritty allies, it should be noted that not having to depend on the commercial or social support of your neighbors for a living—as do business people, elected officials and such—gives one an enviable freedom to speak his mind without fear of financial repercussion. As Guthrie phrased it for a visiting Texas newspaperman, "We [he and Carol] are pariahs. . . . But you see, I don't have to give a damn." (That statement, incidentally, was not only quoted out of context by the Lone Star reporter, but also was positioned in his story in such a way as to suggest something other than what Guthrie was saying.)

For his part, Guthrie doesn't like seeing area ranchers take such an inflexible, anthropocentric stance toward a problem that is in some part their own fault. He feels that before resorting to killing bears that wander down from the mountains in search of food, Front Range ranchers should clean up their feedlots and take greater care locating and using the "boneyards" where they dispose of livestock carcasses.

In personal letters of December 1986 and June 1987, Guthrie wrote, "These boneyards and their heavy smell serve as bait to attract the bears, especially when an east wind blows, carrying the odor of carrion from plains to mountains. . . . Finally, I hold it not coincidental but a case of cause and effect that bears began coming out of the mountains to the Choteau country soon after a commercial feedlot was established north of the town."

Guthrie also asks that ranchers "stop thinking so much of their cash registers" and extend their concerns beyond their personal welfare to the national posterity and the value of preserving what is left of lower-48 wilderness—with which Montana is singularly blessed, and of which the grizzly is the most impressive living representative.

Finally, Guthrie feels that wildlife management authorities, both federal and local, should be given more cooperation and space in which to work out solutions. (In one public meeting in Choteau, for example, visiting wildlife managers were rudely shouted down as they attempted to present ideas for safely accommodating both large numbers of livestock and a few grizzlies along the Front Range.)

Allow now a momentary aside from our theme to present a current view of the grizzly situation in Guthrie's neighborhood, as seen through the eyes of regional wildlife management authorities. In late April of 1987, I spoke with Bill Thomas, Information Officer for the Montana Department of Fish, Wildlife and Parks (FWP). I asked Thomas for an update on grizzly problems and proposed management solutions along the Front.

He replied that FWP has formulated and put into action a contingency plan for special "damage-control" hunts designed to take out, individually and only as necessary, grizzlies that kill livestock.

FWP's definition of predacious grizzlies includes: (a) animals that have killed livestock in the past, were trapped and relocated but have returned to the area and again are causing problems; and (b) excess boars—that is, male bears that have turned to livestock predation and can be eliminated without damaging the reproductive capabilities of the local grizzly population. (The reproductive health of any geographically isolated bear population, as most these days are, depends primarily on the number of breeding-age females, or sows, in that population. As boars are both promiscuous and highly mobile, a few will do.)

From the 1,300 applications submitted for the damage-control hunts, the names of five hunters were drawn. The winning hunters have been notified to be ready to jump at a moment's notice. Should a grizzly predation problem arise and the animal be identified as an offender prone to recidivism, the first of the five hunters on the list will be called and allowed, under supervision, to kill the bruin.

While "hunting" is hardly an appropriate word for what are almost certain to be—in both effect and fact—sportless, challengeless executions, the FWP plan nonetheless is as fair a compromise as has yet been devised. Further, the plan has proven acceptable—at least on a trial basis—to the majority of concerned stockmen, conservationists, hunters and the general public. If no more livestock predation problems arise, or if the problems appear to be amenable to trapping and relocation, then no grizzlies will be killed.

None of this, of course, weakens or destroys Guthrie's argument that as long as ranchers continue to dispose of dead livestock in ways that amount ot bear baiting, hungry grizzlies will continue to be lured down from the mountains by the smell of rotting flesh borne on the winds. Although the FWP plan appears to be a fair and effective, if harsh, treatment of *symptoms*, Guthrie's suggestion for eliminating the most significant probable *causes* still seems to hold the greatest promise for long-term peace along the Front.

But the best spokesman for A. B. Guthrie, Jr.'s views on the grizzly bear and its human foes is neither this observer nor any other, but the man himself. In addition to the *Choteau Acantha* letter reproduced at the opening of this chapter, "Requiem for Old Ephraim" and "The Grizzly Bear Syndrome," both included in Part II, are eloquent messages.

A. B. GUTHRIE, JR.'S
VANISHING
PARADISE

In the summer of 1983, a television crew arrived in Choteau to film a documentary. Titled *A. B. Guthrie, Jr.'s Vanishing Paradise*, the half-hour film, first aired on PBS stations in 1984, provides a sparkling tribute to Guthrie's literature, his land and the man himself.

As evidenced by the title, Guthrie's environmental concerns are central to the film's theme. At one point, after suggesting that the word "change" is more accurate than "progress" for describing what has happened to the West since the arrival of Europeans, Guthrie comments: "If I were to rewrite the Book of John, I would say, 'In the beginning was the Word, and the Word was *Change*.'"

In 1985, Guthrie appeared in a second film dedicated to the preservation of what remains pristine in the West. *A Path to America's Wilderness* was produced by the Bob Marshall Foundation, a nonprofit organization of volunteers working to maintain the integrity of the lower 48's largest designated wilderness area by supplementing restricted federal funding and labor. The Bob Marshall Wilderness, set aside in 1939 and comprising more than a million acres, has been called, and is in fact, the flagship of designated wildlands in the lower 48 states.

One of the Bob Marshall Foundation's primary concerns, and the thrust of their film, is to encourage more Americans, both groups and individuals, to give of their time and money to help rebuild and maintain the Bob's sadly deteriorated hiking and horse-packing trails—trails in some stretches so deeply eroded that the mud-choked run-off of rain and melting snow washes down them in torrents that threaten to sully the crystalline waters of the area's principal western drainage, the South Fork of the Flathead River.

With the Bob's eastern border lying not far beyond the western flank of Ear Mountain, the area is held close to Guthrie's heart and heaven. To help the foundation get moving on its trail-renovation project, he donated his time to travel to the shooting location to narrate both the opening and closing scenes of the 44-minute film.

Excerpts from that narration:

"Man needs space. He needs elbow room. He needs to be surrounded, when he can, by majesty. By the majesty of the mountains. By the majesty of the rivers. By the majesty of wildlife. These things are part of our heritage and should be preserved.

"Though I suppose I won't get here again, that does not diminish the delight I take in knowing the Bob Marshall Wilderness is here . . . something pristine that still exists in America."

To close the film, Guthrie gave from memory a recitation of his poem "Remembering A Man."

You should have known Bob Marshall,
though at first you found him strange.
A youthful man of good appearance,
he chose to live his life alone,
alone among the mountains and the streams.
He found lift and wonder there,
his eyesight sharp for nature's creatures,
his hearing keen for earth's wild songs.
He returned to write his passions
and, that done, set forth again.
In time his spirit lifted us.

We put a million acres in his name
and ruled it wilderness.
You should have known Bob Marshall.

For all his talent, success and recognition, A. B. Guthrie, Jr. today remains a modest, even jokingly self-effacing man. "By modern standards," he quips, "I don't have any of the qualifications to be considered a great writer: I've never spent a night in a drunk tank, I've never been committed to a mental institution, I've never beat up on a woman, and my signature isn't illegible."

The physical man is beginning to show the wear of the years: Since early 1986 an oxygen concentrator has hummed away, part-time, in the Barn. When he travels, he takes an oxygen tank with him, though he uses it sparingly. "The doctors don't say so, but I suppose it's 65 years of smoking that shortens my breath," he told me.

But inside that aging frame still thrives a young man's wit, as sharp-edged and brilliant as an obsidian point. By way of example, in 1985, during the filming of the Bob Marshall documentary, Gary McLean, archaeologist for the Flathead National Forest and one of the film's producers, stood listening to Guthrie talk extemporaneously to the camera. When Guthrie had finished, McLean recalls, Carol Guthrie, standing nearby, exclaimed, "Buddy, you're speaking in perfect paragraphs!" Without pause to reflect, Guthrie, grinning, fired back, "I *think* in perfect paragraphs!"

When I asked Guthrie if there was a message he'd like to leave with his readers at the conclusion of this biographical sketch, he said, "Just tell them I'm still ticking and that I'll continue to write as long as my wits stay with me."

His wife objected: "It's the other way around, Buddy—you'll keep your wits as long as you continue to write."

"Well," Bud Guthrie said, his eyes sparkling. "Well . . ."

THE
ENVIRONMENTAL
ESSAYS OF
A. B. GUTHRIE, JR.

EDITOR'S INTRODUCTORY NOTE

The 22 essays collected here span nearly half a century, from 1939 to 1987, and include the texts of speeches, narratives written to accompany slide and film presentations, newspaper editorials, magazine articles, congressional testimony and prefaces to the books of other conservation writers. Additionally, Guthrie has provided a foreword, written in May 1987, which brings up to date several environmental issues raised in the earlier essays.

It should be pointed out that, of the lot, only a few of the 22 essays have titles created by Guthrie himself. Some were titled by editors of the publications in which they originally appeared. Others, including several of the speeches, were titled by the editor of this collection.

Concerning such editing: In a few instances, brief sections that stood verbatim in two or more essays—historical anecdotes used in speeches, for the most part—have been deleted after their first appearance. Otherwise, the essays appear here virtually word for word, comma for comma, as A. B. Guthrie, Jr. wrote them.

A FOREWORD
TO THE
COLLECTION

Events have dated some of the observations made herein, but I have no reason to soften or divert the thrust of what I have said or written at earlier times.

I hear no talk of the sawfly these days, and block farming, at least in my area, has not succeeded strip mining. There is one exception of sorts. That is what is called sod-busting, which is not block farming really, but rather the turning over by plow of thousands on thousands of acres of indifferent crop land for the sake of profits made possible by government outlays. Abandoned, this soil, that which hasn't blown away, will grow up in weeds. Cultivated, it would yield no profit.

Saline seep, the emergence of acids from the subsoil as a consequence of irrigation and summer fallowing, has been recognized as a growing problem in late years.

The Anaconda Copper Company has sold its Montana daily newspapers since one of the included articles was written. The papers are better as a result. They print more news and in the news columns do not avoid the controversial or the politically inexpedient as the Anaconda press certainly did. At the same time, under the chain ownership that has succeeded copper company control, the papers are lacking in personality or character. Editorially they tend to be neutral, silent on issues that call for strong voices. For a time the *Missoulian* set a brave and stirring example. Then caution overcame courage, and the *Missoulian* fell back among the emasculated. I call the present practice "tiptoe journalism." The editors, or more likely the business managers, tiptoe to the waters of controversy, dip a toe in to test the currents and, thinking of the bottom line, tiptoe away.

Examples are numerous, but I shall cite just one. When our eastern-district congressman suggested that the rules and regulations having to do with clean air and clean water be relaxed for the sake of progress, jobs and prosperity, I read no editorial protest, though God knows that without thought of what we are facing we are doomed. I must admit that my reading was not thorough. There may have been a protest or two, but I'll have to be shown. Montana papers are not much concerned with the environment. Leave that to the columnists, if needs be.

It is interesting that all Montana political figures of real standing have come from western Montana—if Helena, on the rim of the Continental Divide, be included. Senators Wheeler, Walsh, Metcalfe, Mansfield and, though hardly in their class, Senator Murray—all came or come from the Western Slope. The best governor in history was Joe Dixon, also a westerner.

I am talking too much about Montana. The issues discussed in this collection are not merely local. They are nationwide, worldwide. What happens when earth is exhausted? What happens when humans, breeding thoughtlessly, become so many as to overwhelm nature's productivity? We do not like to think of universal hunger and the excesses of behavior that hunger and crowding give rise to. And the result is that we do not take due precautions against that calamity.

Speak of the ozone layer, and how many know what is meant? Speak of acid rain, and how many away from the blight really care? Speak of noxious herbicides and pesticides, and the answer is crops and rural prosperity.

I am being too doleful. Salvation is possible. The hope lies in young people and, I believe, in the old, who have witnessed what change has wrought. We can save what we have not destroyed. We can remedy that which we've hurt. I can believe, I dare to believe that the media—the press, radio and television—will come to face what the world faces and that readers and hearers will respond.

James Thurber chose for a title, *My World—and Welcome to It.* Let's say, instead, "Our World—and Come all ye Faithful."

—A. B. GUTHRIE, JR.
The Barn, Choteau, Montana
May 21, 1987

This brief but poignant essay appeared as an editorial in the Lexington Herald-Leader *for Sunday, January 1, 1939, under the headliner "Faulconer's Eagle." A. B. Guthrie, Jr. recalls the piece as his premiere conservation essay. Two subsequent Guthrie editorials on the same theme appeared in the* Leader *later in the same month.*

ON THE
DEATH OF
AN EAGLE

All night the great bird drooped in a tree, sick with a bullet in her.

At dusk, a marksman made breathless by the size and rarity of her had caught her through his sights, and, wounded, she had risen clumsily and planed painfully away on pinions that had fanned a thousand miles of airways on the food-quest to Kentucky.

And now a flock of silly crows, excited by her bulk and aspect, gathered round to scream at her. In other days she would have cast off from the limb and fled the braggart scolding, but now she sat quiet, her fierce eyes fading with the pain in her.

The clamor of the crows had its message for the marksman, who had risen before dawn with the blood-hunger strong in his hunter's heart. In the pearl of early morning he crept up, and now he had her fair on the bead again and his finger bore on the trigger.

Later, he lifted her up and spread the folded wings and let his picture be taken thus, a hunter with his trophy, while the strong, bold head of the bird hung limp against the ruff of her breast.

He will mount the eagle, will Baily Faulconer, and stand it in the county supply plant, and people who see it will know what a golden eagle looks like. That is, they will know what a golden eagle with glass eyes looks like set dead and stiff in a room. Maybe they will never know the majesty and grace and flowing power of a live eagle, they are becoming so rare!

This essay is taken from an article Guthrie wrote for the November 1949 issue of The Writer *magazine. That article, in turn, was based on a lecture delivered in August of the same year at the prestigious Bread Loaf Writers' Conference.*

CHARACTERS
& COMPASSION

I'm going to talk about characterization—not very much on the technique of it but on the content, the source of it, without which technique is no good at all.

I'll start out with a personal experience.

A few weeks ago I was in the mountains of Montana, at a summer cabin just four miles away from a small dude ranch. This has been a dry year in Montana. Up in the hills the usual crop of wild fruit, of raspberries and chokecherries and strawberries, has been scant. As a consequence, a black bear, driven down from the highlands by hunger, had taken to raiding the garbage cans at the dude ranch. Shots fired over his head didn't scare him away for long. Morning and night he appeared again to paw over the leavings in the cans.

The dude rancher didn't want to kill him. Anyhow, it's against the law to do so except in actual emergencies. And at the same time he was worried lest one of his guests blunder into the bear at night.

So he called the Wildlife Service and asked for help. The Wildlife Service sent a man up.

Now it happened that I was there, a nonpaying guest at the place, when the man arrived.

He was a young man, long and lean, with a face that looked as if it liked to kill things. He had a brand-new .270 Remington that he showed me with pride, wiping the prints of my fingers from the blued-steel barrel after I had handled it.

He also had a bear trap, a heavy, spring trap with hooked teeth, capable, he said, of holding a 1,200-pound animal. He set it in back of the lodge, and posted signs for travelers to keep away. Around the trap he threw a few pieces of beef scrap.

We went back to the cabin then and had dinner—supper, we call it in Montana—and the gang got to telling stories and singing songs while the darkness fell.

It was about 10:30 p.m. when the cook, back in the kitchen, heard the clank of the trap. She came running in to tell us, and the lean, hard young man leaped to his feet and grabbed up his shiny rifle and asked me to come along with the flash. He told the others to stay back. You couldn't tell, he said, the bear might break out of the trap, even out of a trap that would hold 1,200 live pounds.

We two stumbled out into the dark and climbed the hill back of the cabin, and there in the light of the flash was the bear. He wasn't making a sound. He wasn't grunting or roaring or squalling at the steel teeth in his leg. He would rear back against the chain spiked into a heavy tree and, failing in that, would rear and bat the trap against the trees around him.

That was what we saw—the bear lunging and rearing and batting the trap against the trees. What we heard was just the clank of the metal and the hard strike of steel on wood.

"Hold the light steady," the young man said.

He brought up his rifle, and for a minute it seemed to me he hesitated, as if somehow unwilling to line up the sights.

Then the rifle barked and the bear slumped down, and we waited to make sure he was good and dead before going closer.

He was. The lean young man had cracked his skull.

We went up after a minute or two, and the young man stooped, and I could see both his actions and the look on his face in the wash of the flash. He put his hand on the bear, gently, and said. "There, boy," and then he turned his young killer's face to me and said, "Goddam such a job, anyhow."

Why do I tell this story? What is the point of it? Can you guess?

It seems to me to have a good many points. I've told it, first of all, to underscore the subject of this article—which is characterization.

What is the manifestation that made this young man a character, a human being, rather than the symbol of blood-thirst? It was the final show of compassion, wasn't it? Now it seems to me that when you hunt bears in fiction—or doves, for that matter, you need to do so with compassion. (You may substitute understanding if you want to. The word "compassion" seems to me nearest to what I mean.) It appears to me that compassion is perhaps the most important single quality, the first requirement of the writer of fiction. Your villain isn't all villain. In degree he's a victim of circumstance. He's rooting in the garbage because the berry crop has failed, like this unhappy stumble-bum of a bear. Or he's shooting because he's had to make a choice, maybe the wrong one, to be sure, like the young hunter.

If we let the bear be the hero of this story, what do we have to know about him, except that hunger has driven him from the hills and into the trap? There's one thing—can you guess it?—that must be added. Well, that if you had happened to stumble into him in the dark, he might have wiped half your face away with a stroke.

So, you regard your characters with compassion—not uncritically, either, mind you. You understand them. You know what makes them tick. You are at once critical and sympathetic, with the consequence that these creatures of your mind emerge full-blown on paper. Without the full understanding, without that compassion, you have one-sided, incredible, flat figures. You have the kind of symbol that the bear hunter seemed to me until I heard him say, "Goddam such a job, anyhow."

The writer, even the established writer, I think, keeps asking himself if he's good enough to write. Is he a good enough human being, that is? Is what he has to say worth saying? Had it better be left unsaid? Authorship carries a responsibility. Words printed, words said, influence minds and hearts, for better or for worse. And so you ask yourself if your attitudes are right. You ask if you are capitalizing on the shallow illusions, the smug moralities, the little conceits, the slick evasions, the respected falsities. You ask if you have the intelligence to see and, seeing, the courage to say. You ask yourself these questions and others, a lot of others. And I would almost say, if the answer is favorable, that it adds up to compassion.

In this essay, excerpted from an article by the same title published in the September 1950 issue of Holiday *magazine, Guthrie comments candidly on his perception of the strengths and weaknesses of Montanans and, thus, Montana.*

MONTANA

Montanans may come closest still to believing that any boy can grow up to be president. The reason seems pretty obvious. So many residents of the Treasure State, coming from the East, coming from Norway, Sweden, Denmark, Germany, Scotland, Ireland, found opportunity waiting. They incline to forget that those were the days of the open range, of free land, undiscovered ore, unclaimed water. They forget that every available acre worth a nickel has been taken up. They made out for themselves, didn't they? Anyone ought to be able to do the same.

The memory of natural riches waiting for the claiming is recent. It accounts not only for this faith in self-determinism but also for the fact that Montanans don't take too much stock in plundered-land talk. The stockman finds it hard to believe that ranges can be overgrazed. All we need is rain, he says, searching the dry, blue sky. He doesn't always realize that once the streams ran clear that now run rusty. He'll agree with an ag-college man I talked to who ventured the opinion that, although trees and cows and people might all die, the native grasses, as natural-selection survivors of the hordes of buffalo, would go on forever. What bothers the stockman is government interference. Lord, how he hates it; except, of course, for the tariff, which doesn't strike him as interference, anyhow.

Elsewhere you find this confidence in the adequacy of resources. Or perhaps you find myopia. The mining man thinks—and maybe rightly—that there's ore in plenty yet, considering the new and more efficient processes of extraction. The sawmill operator wants new roads to standing timber; there's no money to be made in stumps.

For a while, until good years and the war and wartime prices came along, it appeared that the dry-land wheat rancher might have learned a lesson. He had had a tough time, for a variety of reasons.

One was that he had watched his topsoil blow into the Dakotas. On occasion, as the fertility of his place dwindled, he had moved from one quarter or half section to another. Advised by experts, encouraged by government payments, he began to strip-farm. The wind did him less damage that way.

But government payments declined. The price of wheat climbed. During the war, production was the thing. More, though wind damage was lessened when wheat was planted in strips, other damage was increased, damage from the grasshopper and the sawfly, which works on the edges of fields and had more edges to work on when crops were stripped.

So strip farming has declined in favor of block farming, and now, after the first bad year in nearly a decade, serious-minded observers are asking if the whole lesson has to be relearned, assuming that it ever was learned.

With more dry years, will the soil blow again, no matter what newfangled gadgets and experimental procedures are used to prevent its blowing? Must we start the long and painful process all over again?

Good years, high prices, reduced government payments and the war discouraged strip farming; they also brought into cultivation acres and acres of marginal land better left in virgin sod. As in the old homestead and desert-entry years, hopeful plowmen turned under the bunch and buffalo grass that cattle and sheep thrive on.

Leaner times will force them to abandon it. Land so left, though, doesn't grow up in bunch and buffalo grass. It grows up in tumbleweeds and Russian thistle and that dubious import, sweet clover.

The pity is that the vegetation thus turned under made perhaps the finest forage in the world.

The Montanan, especially the old-timer, is apt to sniff and ask what things are coming to. Physically his world is large; population-wise it is small. He gets a look at things. Both the largeness and the smallness affect him. He finds it hard to imagine a crowded world, difficult to think of humanity *en masse*. And so, I might add, would you. This is a different world from the Midwest and East. Different circumstances bear on judgment. You feel isolated, happily isolated, free of the frets of our time. Let the world go hang. It is at this point that you need to remind yourself that we tried to let it go hang before.

Part of the citizenry is glad that the ratio of space to population is high. They don't want a lot of outlanders to people the unpeopled places, to fish out the trout streams and spoil the hunting. Another part wants to promote the state, but even the promoters, like the Montana Chamber of Commerce, speak rather cautiously of small, home-owned industry that would help to solve the seasonal unemployment problem. With syndicate operations and mechanization growing both on farms and in lumber areas, they foresee even fewer seasonal jobs.

A passionate expatriate Montanan like me asks himself what binds him to the state. Is it just my interest in a time and activity? Is it scenery, space, the opportunity for solitude? Is it friends? Is it old and rich associations with places and with people?

It is these: It is the riffle of the west wind in the redtop. It is a pack trail to the Chinese Wall and the Continental Divide. It is a horseman and a bronc. It is limpid fishing streams like the Madison and the Flathead and Sun River and the Teton. It is a round of ditchwater whiskies with old-timers who by and by will get to reminiscing. It is the aching roll of badlands. It is the girls, the lithe young girls, goldened by the blood of Scandinavia, coppered by the touch of *voyageur* and Indian. It is the cool summer nights with the coyotes crying.

But Montana is something more than anything said so far. It is something else, something that makes others love the state though they recognize its shortcomings, that gives to visitors the sense of living in a different, a less fretful, and a better world. It is, as I think I've already indicated, that here one feels an individual superiority to event, a be-damned attitude toward mischance, a freedom from or ascendancy over the anxieties that press so hard elsewhere. Montanans somehow stay on top of life.

A rancher I know lived in town. He had a great wheat-crop prospect one year—600 acres standing thick, almost ready for the combine and the elevator. Wheat was selling high, almost three dollars a bushel. The ranch foreman came to the house early one morning. He roused the rancher, to tell him hail had felled every straw during the night.

"Oscar," the rancher said, "why'd you want to wake me up to tell me this? There's plenty of time to worry when I'm ready to get up." With that he turned over and went back to sleep.

I know the man. I know he'd do it. He's pure Montana, out of Norway.

The following essay is taken from an article by the same title, which Guthrie wrote for the July 1955 issue of Holiday *magazine.*

THE

ROCKIES

buy the West. I buy it place and person, body and soul—if not with blind affection, still with an honest and enduring affection. It is home.

I mean the Rocky Mountain West. I mean the states of Montana, Idaho, Wyoming, Colorado and Utah and, less surely because of less intimate acquaintance, Nevada, Arizona and New Mexico. I mean the land of cactus and cattle, of sagebrush and sheep and wind-harried wheat, of snowy heights, of physical immensity and social microcosm, of history murmurous at the back door, of blizzard and chinook and coyotes crying to the night.

Easterners, save those whom necessity keeps from returning, either haven't experienced or can't sufficiently appreciate the values here. Nor can or have West Coasters. The coastal states aren't West, even if the compass points that way. They boast great, mushrooming cities and strange interests and populations unrelated to wagon trains and steamboats on the mad Missouri. Though never so west as the states just to the east, they have moved far from their origins, out of the old day into a new. Young, they call themselves, but their growth and change are only age come swiftly.

Mine is the young land, the young, raw, hardy land, though such are the uses of words that men call it the Old West. Old? Old only because it holds close to the days of its youth. Old because new is a name for today—which, when you think of it, is older than yesterday.

Call my West anachronistic. Call it unprogressive. Call it rude. It is still mine. Some of the reasons are obscure, and some can't be defined at all, and still others may be unreasonable, but it is still mine.

To East and West Coast both, the Rockies are a physical divide. But they are a divide, too, between peoples, between habits of thought, between directions of outlook, and they have their own divisive culture, distinct as those to east and west. Once beyond their great barrier, the Forty-Niner and the traveler to Oregon, like their modern successors, had left the East behind in a degree beyond awareness. Eastward was The Wall; westward, while they mined and planted, was the open sea and Orient. Walled off from their wandering brothers, Easterners kept gazing east. Tardily between them came the settlers of the Rockies. It is an over-simplification but an expression of substantial truth to say the West Coaster looked west, the East Coaster looked east, and the man of the Rockies just looked around. There was plenty to see. And, despite trains, trucks, convertibles and planes, it is no less accurate to say they still do.

Fur brought the first white men in numbers, beaver fur, largely, which was used in the making of hats for the smart gentry of England. They came up the Missouri, these traders and trappers, assisted by French rivermen who were half beaver themselves, and they put up their posts and set out their traps and with whisky traded the Indians out of what peltries they had. Or they journeyed overland across the wide plains, along a route soon to be known as the Oregon Trail, and topped the backbone of the continent and dropped down to Green River, where beaver were thick beyond thinking. Or they took the still older trace that would take them, God willing, to Santa Fe.

Only the daring set forth, and only the hardy and lucky survived. These ranged far and wide, equal to weather and Indians and solitudes such as to orphan the soul. Like one Osborne Russell, they pulled through while horses froze in their tracks. Like Jim Bridger and Kit Carson, they survived the arrows and muskets of Blackfeet and Bannocks and Sioux.

Like John Colter, the first white man to thread that hell land later named Yellowstone Park, they tried fearful wilderness.

Ranging, they scorned more and more the cramped life of the settlements. Here were beaver and buffalo and the good tingle of danger, and no clock to watch, no crop to plant, no counter to tend, no chores to do. Just yonder was prime meat for the shooting, and the yonder creek water to drink. What if the camp lacked for bread and for salt? A fur hunter lost his taste for such stuff. Here, for a fact, was the way for a man. Here was the free way for free men.

Admit they were not tame to begin with, else they wouldn't have been there. The circumstances of a wild life made them still wilder. Loneliness and hazard and day-by-day unpredictability undo the moralities, and these men, though by choice, were lonely most of the time, imperiled often, and subject always to chance. A broken leg or the loss of a horse or an arrow from nowhere could bring death to a man, to any man no matter how careful. Like the turns of the sharp-turning weather, life was a gamble, perhaps to be lost to a fellow fur hunter offended in a moment of fun, to a man, that is, like yourself. You never could tell.

So they lived in their way while they could, looking ahead as they trapped lonesome streams to the annual visit of traders out of St. Louis, to the big shindig, the fracas, the spree known as *rendezvous*, where whisky and squaws would be plenty and gamblers game as could be. They shot the works then, on the Wind or the Green. They drank up their pelts and lost them at contests and cards, for what was money but beaver and what was beaver but lots more in the streams? Now and at other times that afforded, they took Indian girls, to leave or, rarely, to keep. They became fathers of children, to forget or, rarely, to care for.

It is easy to fault them, to call them wanton and profligate and thoughtless of tomorrow and God. Too easy. These were great men in their way, and their way was the way of courage and resource, if also the way of the undisciplined wild, as it became in the nature of things. We are deep in their debt, though they served us unconsciously and rued the results. They were the pathfinders, the trail breakers, the spade men for America's westering. Who but they, for foremost example, discovered South Pass, that break in the great solid wall of the Rockies through which thousands of home seekers were later to labor?

They didn't last long. Thirty years or so. By 1842, less than four decades after Lewis and Clark had dared the unknown, the great life largely was over. Paradise frazzled out into wretched and transient remainders—buffalo-hide hunting, wolfing, piloting pilgrims and soldiers. To this day, along river courses beavered again, you can hear the echoes of their sunset:

"It's them nabob British, wantin' silk hats now and not beaver. So who's to pay fat for fine fur?"

"I swear, beaver's been sceerce, though, and I call to mind when every lift of the trap brought up a prime plew."

"The country's sp'ilin', I'm thinkin'. Looky that passel of greenhorns we hear's bound for South Pass. This ain't a place for pilgrims and plows."

It was, though. A lot of it was, now that the mountain men had been there.

For a few years, then, the building of Western character slowed down. A different kind of man toiled the routes the fur hunter had found, a gentler kind made gentler yet by the presence of wives and children. Not for them the stern mountains and the stern climate. Not for them, even, the upland deserts, which, they reasoned, must always be the abode of nomadic barbarians. These heights, these wastes were merely obstacles, though formidable ones, inserted between regions fit for human habitation. Beyond the sky-high, no-end-to-it wall of the mountains, on the lower Columbia, on the Willamette, was a life like the one they had left in Missouri or Maine except that through the bounty of Providence it would be incredibly richer. The soil was the thing, the fertile Far-Western soil, waiting there to be grubbed and turned over and fenced, and so made into the cozy assurance of a person's identity in the lost flow of space.

We need not remain with them long. If not by comparison with the trapper, they were bold men, too, bolder at least than the kinsmen and friends who wouldn't leave home. These lower-Columbia farmers, these jumpers of half a continent and more, left between East and Pacific the final frontier, the Mountain West. If a last frontier exists, this is it.

The lag in the casting of character. The lag, and then, the resumption.

Gold got it going again, gold struck in the late '50s and '60s even as fresh parties of grangers deepened the Oregon Trail. Gold high on the South Platte where Denver was to be born, gold in Nevada, on the Orofino in Idaho, at Bannack, Alder Gulch and Last Chance in Montana.

Prudence doesn't chase after nuggets or set up gambling halls and saloons in unruly and probably impermanent camps. It stays safe at home and counts wealth already minted while keeping an eye out for more. So, as before, it was the rashlings who set forth, this time for the mountains with shovels and pans or maybe a monte deck and a barrel. Call them the stout or foolhardy, the daring or reckless, the ambitious or disreputable. In natural bent they were kin to the fur hunter. Gold wasn't so different from beaver. It was something to spend, and there was lots more where it came from.

While they panned dust and spent it, an enterprise new to the mountains and soon to be more important than mining got a start near the diggin's. Cattle trailed into the camps, it was found, flourished on the sparse grasses of high plain and valley. They could, or so it came to appear, survive the hard winters without hay or grain. Here was a new kind of gold then, gold on the hoof, gold that would fatten and multiply on the endless free swards of the West.

Few ways of life lasted long in the West, but while it lasted the life of the range, like the life of the earlier trapper, was the life for a sure-enough man, for a man who liked freedom with a touch of excitement and a good pinch of danger, for the man who liked to look far, knowing he could pull stakes and go there whenever he pleased. Ranch life in the winter could be dull, no doubt about that; but always, at the end of the season or trail, if not by good fortune sooner, there was a town where a man fully made up for what he had lacked in the way of horseplay, gaming, women and drink. It is worthy of note how close this life was except for the method of livelihood, to the earlier life of the trapper. Both lived free and easy, as had the gold miner in turn.

So thousands of cattle were brought to the northern ranges from Eastern Oregon, Eastern Washington and Texas, brought in the nice expectation that they could get through the winters just by grazing the grass that had cured on the stem. They did for a while, with the consequence that thousands more were trailed in. Then came the winter of '86-'87. It was such a time as even old-timers professed never to have experienced, though they probably had; a winter of long, bitter cold, snowstorm on snowstorm, ice flintlike over the browse. Men house-bound and impotent had to watch while bone-skinny cows, lowing forlornly, fell down and died from cold and starvation. Not many were left when spring came around. Ranchers reported 50-percent losses, 75, losses virtually total. Carcasses covered the coulees.

That winter broke men and outfits and brought about a change: no real northern rancher today would dream of making out without feed. But the adjustment of methods is not the important thing. The important thing is that nature had shown again how extreme she could be and so how open to chance was life in the West. Open both ways, for that matter, to good luck and bad, for hadn't ranch winters been kind enough prior to this granddaddy of winters? Broke today. Maybe rich tomorrow.

All right, maybe broke again the day after. That was the way of things. That was the climate.

Later developments, bewailed and resisted by don't-fence-me-in men, nevertheless supported the pattern. The homesteader came with his plows and his wire, often at first to find the skies gracious and then unaccountably and incredibly cruel. The chinook that rejoiced him in winter, he learned, scorched his grain in July. June rain by next June could be drought. Wind could shatter out wheat, hail pound it into the ground, early snow flatten it beyond reach of the cutter bar. A hundred and sixty wasn't enough. Maybe not 320. Maybe not anything, for the more a man spent the farther he went in the hole.

Back then and since then, producing wheat and cattle in these mountained plains has been just another roll of the ball, and where she stops nobody knows. She stopped on the double naught during the depression and badly bent the men she didn't break. Since then she's paid off handsomely. The needs of wars, hot or cold, a long-time cycle of generally favorable weather, government aid of one sort and another—these have filled the pockets of wheat ranchers and cattlemen, or would have filled them had not the beneficiaries liked so well to celebrate the shining hour.

Possibly no other people are so pleased with place as residents of this inland West. But ask a Westerner what's so great about the West, and he'll say, maybe, the mountains or the streams or fish and game or the spirit of the people or maybe even the climate which cured his asthma. The list of treasures seldom will be ordered or complete.

What really captivates the Western man is living room, for most of what he values comes from it. A large degree of privacy. A sort of spatial insulation from other human animals. He can go out and listen to silence. He can picnic without having to mix with picnicking strangers. He can get to work quickly, to fields and streams quickly. He doesn't have to ride subways or commuters' trains. He doesn't have to crane to see ahead or rig up a penthouse for a view of the skyline. His children, idled from school, don't have to have play planned and supervised—for there, right there, is the open and healthful and entertaining outdoors.

All is well, then, or all would be well if it weren't for a contradiction that leaves a great many Westerners split down the middle. Growth is the rule of nature. It means more jobs, more people, better business—but maybe an end and certainly a restriction of the good life. The conflict finds some men on one side and some on the other, but largely it goes on within the individual himself. The saddened observer of living room already reduced may be the chairman of a committee to attract factories.

The progressives see, or profess to, a great development of the Mountain West, a development barely suggested as yet. Within the Rocky Mountains' eight states are 42.6 percent of the coal reserves of the nation, 100 percent of the oil shale, 7.1 percent of the petroleum reserves. The coal alone is sufficient for 1000 years. Within 20 years, the shale may be yielding as much as 2 million barrels of oil daily. And what of potash and phosphate? What of uranium and atomic energy? What of power development, irrigation, reclamation? Oh, yes, the West has a destiny and the West is on the way.

But I remember pack trips in the mountains and a stream talking near my bed and the all-well tolling of the bell mare's bell and the moon like a ripe fish egg where the high hills shored the sky; and nowhere was there anyone, not anyone but the people of our little company, snugged down for the journey through the night. It had been a good day. We had caught fish and seen the utter purity of sego lilies and the sprayed pride of beargrass and, in a burn, the flame of fireweed. High on a shelf a wild goat floated like a piece of cloud. We had come back to camp tired with a good tiredness and had scorched the supper trout and offered the platter with apologies to Ray Gibler, our guide and friend, and he had answered characteristically, "I'm like a graveyard; I'm atakin' anything."

And I remember nights on the plains when the wind whispered in the grass and you could reach a star and a wing fanned unseen overhead. A man felt wonderfully small with the miles rolling away and away from him into the last ranks of shadow, felt insignificant and fine, felt gathered into himself, a tiny unity against the great diversity, or felt dispersed, aflow with space, and was happy at that too.

And once we lunched in sagebrush, in a million square miles of sagebrush, in nothing but sagebrush except for the far, far blue of Western mountains; and my small girl child, used to the steel and stone of civilization, spread her arms and cried, "This is beautiful. This is the most beautiful place in the world." It was. In that moment, it was.

I am not sad with memories, though. If I can't recapture old experiences, I still can find others of like kind. In my West I can. There is a cliff there, rising sheer, and, beyond, the great snowed head of Pentagon or Pike or Teewinot. Here is a lake, matched blue to sky, where trout make spreading rings; here a white-green grove of aspens where baneberry bleeds and Indian paintbrush blows; here and on and on from here a sweep of plain on which a far butte waves. Summer dusk creeps on, the hour of quiet, of no wind, and the sun notches itself in the high hills and slides away, letting night smoke the eastward slopes and leaving such a glory in the sky as to make a man imagine he is within mind-hold, almost, of essence.

Men before me have looked and felt a heady ownership. Other men do so now. Still others will do so after death extinguishes our right. For ours is an ownership of things that know no ownership. The Rockies belong to any and to all who have an eye and heart for them, to all whose spirits lift with mountains and sail with sailing space.

This essay is taken from a piece by the same title that ran in the July 1958 issue of Holiday, *where the words of A. B. Guthrie, Jr. were accompanied by the photographs of Ansel Adams.*

OUR

LORDLY

MOUNTAINS

In the wild million acres of the Bob Marshall Wilderness area in Montana there is a spot called Danaher. Only guides and sportsmen and men of the Forest Service know it, for it is just a camping place. It has no post office, no store, no permanent residents. But it does have a story.

Fifty years and more ago an Irishman named Tom Danaher secured patent to 160 acres deep in these mountains. To his homestead he took building materials, household equipment, ranch machinery. Moreover, the lore of the region has it, he even imported a piano. Let us embrace the report, whether fact or legend, for all the rest is true.

In many another place many another man has supplied the wants of home and field, but here there was a difference. Every piece of planking, every mouthful of processed food, every pot and sickle and bull wheel and frame, the piano in its indivisible bulk and heft—all had to be packed in by horse or mule, without wagon or cart.

Imagine if you can. The long, long way from the settlements of Lincoln or Ovando. The trail twisting in the timber, wading watercourses, snaking up and down the pitches. The struggling pack string. The heavy awkwardness of the piano slung between two mules in single file. Old Tom Danaher adjusting packs, chopping deadfall, helping ease his cargo through squeeze, past yawning underhang, until at last he was home, home in his mountains, home with his supplies and his tools and his music.

Maybe you can see him there while the tired pack animals, free of their burdens, roll to relieve their sweaty backs, and coyotes cry their evening chorus. It is the hour of no wind. Westward the mountains cut scallops in the fading sky. There is work still to do, but for a moment he stands, fatigued yet exhilarated, looking and listening, breathing deep. Now, here, if I may borrow what someone said before me, he has room to swing his elbows and his mind.

Tom Danaher has been dead for years, and his land has gone back to public domain, and few visitors know how the place got its name. But old-timers remember, and at Ovando or Lincoln they'll tell you, "Tom Danaher? Ah, there was a real mountain man!"

In the 1920s, at the University of Montana at Missoula, a coed named Elsie A. McDowall took mountains and her mood among them as the subject of a poem. She was, so to speak, on the scene of operations, for Missoula lies in a bowl. About her rose the shapes of Mt. Sentinel and Jumbo, the broken steeps of the Rockies and the Bitterroots and, farther on, the high shards called the Missions. Perhaps with misgivings, perhaps with assurance she started out:

> I'm sitting on the hill and all around
> The grey of twilight whitens on the grass . . .

After a few more lines of establishment she went on:

> And I have eager thoughts, and eager hopes,
> And strange, strong longings, and I cast them all
> Into the sky to center round the moon
> And take grand shapes about the rough horizon,
> While all I do is sit and look and look
> And see the hidden stuff out of my life
> And out of books and from my neighbors' lives
> Take form and meaning, depth and grandeur there. . . .

Succeeding lines have a better place in a later connection. To the point, here is the name she gave her poem: "My Life Lies Grand Among the Hills."

Years and arthritis are beginning to afflict a professional packer and guide who is a friend of mine. With greater and greater effort, though still with a competence that makes the greenhorn marvel, he takes his pack strings and his dudes into the high Sun River country or over the Divide to the waters of the Flathead or, by fancy or request, just about wherever man and horse can go.

Out of concern I asked him tactlessly not long ago, "What will you do when these mountains grow too much for you?"

With only outward jocularity he answered, "Come that time, I guess I can always find a tree that's willin' to fall on me."

These illustrations are local, but their application is continental and more. Wherever mountains are, there exist people to whom mountains are where life should be lived. To millions more they are a fascination, an exhilaration, a challenge, a solace; but when a man tries to state why, he finds himself using the impotent abstractions. Like magnificence. Like solitude. Like self-humility. Like freedom and beauty. Or he goes the other way and speaks of fresh air and fishing, of bighorn and bear. None of these suffices, and together they don't explain. Maybe we can't improve on the simple statement that mountains are mountains.

Add to the statement, incidentally but relevantly, that they are incomparable except to other mountains—a fact which helps to account for our stuttering descriptions. You may liken a steamship or a skyscraper or a wrestler to a mountain, but hardly the reverse, though we do it. Our peaks we call Baldys or Bears or Castles or, in the case of a height that rises hard by my cabin, Ear Mountain. None is descriptive, each is diminishing. Even that far-sounding name, the Grand Tetons, sounds tiny, sounds like the blurt of an inflamed mind, when you stand breathless in that sky-high company. *Teton*, a French word, means a woman's breast.

I have visited the ranges of the Appalachians from the Cumberlands to the Greens. I have traveled the Adirondacks and Black Hills and Cascades and seen the great domes of Shasta and Hood and Adams and St. Helens. It is not ignorance or prejudice but circumstance that inclines me to the northwest Rockies, for I know them best.

Our cabin rests high on the apron of the main range, close to Montana's Teton River, not much more than a day's pack trip to the Continental

Divide, which here we call the Chinese Wall. Close to the kitchen is a pond, or lake as we in Montana term any body of water which gives room for a duck's descent.

In the morning and evening, before and after my stint at the typewriter, I leave the cabin to take a look outside, for now is the time of movement. Like me, I can believe almost, my fellow creatures are taking time for fun. In the mown grass a cottontail skips, stops, watches and, watching, snips a leaf from my currant bush with a disdainful and delicate competence. Overhead a Clark's nutcracker cracks a nut. But my first glance, before I set out for a walk, tends toward the lake, where I see feeding trout nose rings, where a beaver may be working or a pair of mallards squawk themselves aloft. It catches the morning and the evening sky, and I think no less of it that it holds a bloodsucker and a toad.

Beyond the aspens lifts an antlered head. A great horned owl sails from the dead branch of a cottonwood. Somewhere magpies hold a caucus. Underfoot, in the protection of the quaking asps, coral root springs like dyed asparagus, and mountain asters and Indian paintbrush blush unseen except by me. Here is the hard red of the baneberry bush, there the soft red of the twinberry. South and west Ear Mountain lifts, a pile, a climb, an aspiration of grim serenity.

No longer do I take a rifle or a shotgun with me, though mine is deer and grouse and small-game country, where you may see a black bear or, by luck, a mountain lion. By short extension it is elk and goat and moose and grizzly country, too, but I go unarmed, pleased by seeing. In my absence visitors hunt against my wishes. Or they go through, bound for prime elk grounds, and come back displaying their dead freight.

I am not too critical. I liked to hunt once and do not know now whether it is maturity or decline that says to let life live, that tells me to forgo the gun in favor of the eye. A kill is a removal and a loss if, like me, you like to watch. For the sight of being and grace it substitutes the sober sight of meat.

I still like to wet a line and see it liven to the rainbow's strike and feel the straining arch of rod and hear the reel's whir. But I'm satisfied to fill the supper pan.

At nights our place is quiet now, except perhaps for the thin call of some bird or the patter of a pine squirrel or chipmunk on the roof. No more do coyotes sing, not even the single one whose single voice, magnified and various, becomes a choir and sends a good and lonesome tingle down the spine. The men of the State Fish and Game Commission and the U. S. Fish and Wildlife Service—the former under the goad of Montana livestock men—have seen to that. Coyotes are predators, they say without public allowance for what useful else they are, and so they've dropped their lethal pellets from aloft; they've flown their sure pursuits and blasted down with scatterguns and rifles. Nor will or can they be satisfied, it seems, scarce though the coyote has become, until the last voice dies.

Bears they kill, too, on suspicion of marauding, mountain lions on suspicion only, bobcats on principle. But the troublesome porcupine and skunk go unmolested. There isn't much glamour in taking to town a load of these.

My adventures, I suppose, are small and quiet ones, though big enough for me. How come a full-grown flicker fell down the flue into my fireplace? How come the same mishap befell a magpie, whose hundred fellows held excited conference outside and adjourned it forthwith when I set him free? What were they saying, these smartest of our birds, gifted of tongue, able with training to utter human speech, while I held within two hands his shining black and white and felt his agitated pulse? *Courage!? Come out!? Don't desert the ship, boys!?* I was and am reminded somehow of the talking down of storm-blind planes.

These landed in the grate, the flicker and the magpie, and, shortly afterwards, a duck, a young but fully feathered bufflehead. His kind lights on water and sometimes on the ground, but never in my knowledge on a perch, and so I couldn't believe he'd sought a roosting place on top the chimney only to falter and fall down. He must be injured then and, unable to go farther, by chance had hit the flue. But when I tried to slide him into the lake, he took wing from my palms.

Others know more of wild adventure, and around campfires or in night cabins they renew the old debate on the most dangerous of animals, the most dangerous, that is, that we know. While the stars listen and the creek clucks to itself regardless, or while the west wind whines outside the house and the wood stove purrs inside, some nominate the grizzly; others, to the astonishment of tyros, name the moose.

"Don't tell me," one old acquaintance says. "Let a grizzly come at you, and you won't have any doubts—that is, if you live. I got respect for him, so much that once I crawled away, seeing one there by the Chinese Wall I was a-scared to shoot, he was so big. Take that case on Sun River just two years ago. That bear was shot and hit and shot and hit who knows how many times, but still he charged and mauled a man and like to bit his head off and, what's more, was stout and fierce enough to rush the rescue party later." The speaker sighs. "It gets me, that young fellow, beat and clawed and tooth-scalped like they say and lying there praying to die and dying before the doc flew in."

"Ah." It's my friend, the guide and packer, answering after a pause. "Use to be, they say, before the West got gentled, that a grizzly bear would tackle you on sight, for no reason except he didn't like your looks. It ain't so any more, or hardly ever. It takes a bullet or some such offense to get his dander up. But a moose, a bull moose, now! He don't need provocation. He's mad to start with, and he can kill you just as dead as any bear. Once, when it was out of season and I didn't have a handy rifle, one charged me there on Basin Creek by Pentagon, and me on horseback too. For half a mile or more he pounded on my tail, and if I hadn't had a steady horse you might never heard the story."

Count as added attractions such told details. In high and open theaters the feature is to look and let the stray thoughts run. To look, alone, with others who have looked at mountains and still others who are looking. In any height to see Monadnock as did Thoreau and Emerson. To look with Robert Frost on Bread Loaf. To take in the tumble of the Smokies and sense about you the absent company of sentiment. To be all by yourself, yet not, to think fresh thoughts, yet not, in the Greens or Blacks or Whites or at the foot of Whitney, Rainier, Yale or Teewinot. To see and feel them close and feel the new-old feelings.

To be with Elsie McDowall there on the hill and with her gaze down and think:

. . .There my meanest deeds,
Ugliest hints of thought and dullest moods
I see detached from me, placed in their place
Like worm scars in a tree. And I feel sad
With pity, but not shame. And my fine deeds,
Pure motives, and true thoughts; they are there, too,
Though no more mine alone, but all the world's,
Resting so widely there upon the hills
Beyond virtue's confines and all merit.
For I'm alone with hills and fields and trees,
And I can feel reality all bare
Against me, and I know, as I am free
From sins now, I am free from virtue, too.
Those mountains are, trees are, and so am I.

And so are we; and here, I think somehow, we find a further explanation for the attraction mountains hold. We speak of majesty, of the good sense of humility, of the comfort to the soul bestowed by solitude. All are valid if not eloquent or complete. In the company of mountains, among the everlasting hills, we are supported and consoled by the thought of permanence, by our impermanent fellowship with permanence. There, here, within a hand's grasp, is immortality. The mountain is, and so am I, forever and forever.

Or so I felt with more assurance once.

Now in his blind ambition man has become a force both geographical and astral, and strange moons sail the sky, and the man in the moon is a frozen dog, and science has discovered in a fist of dust power enough to make dust of our mountains. The fellowship may be a fellowship of transients.

But still I look across the tough grass of the bench, beyond the muscled jackpine, past the lively Teton River, yonder to the foot and climb and summit of Ear Mountain, and I can tell myself that it will last awhile.

DEAR

JOE

ear Joe:

They want me to write a piece about you and your first book.

I wish I could talk it out in the way you and I used to talk in those long bull sessions in Lexington and Missoula and Great Falls, not to mention the Teton canyon where the sight of your old cabin always reminds me of them.

I'd like people to know you outside your book, which, for all its qualities, humor included, may suggest by its rightful force of conviction that you had little fun in your system. That would miss the mark a mile. You always were fun, in agreement and disagreement, in Kentucky or Montana or wherever, over mint juleps or ditchwaters. You were fun, even, when you shook my conservatism with a grin or a crack.

I'd like readers to know, too, that you weren't forever chasing causes, that you could enjoy the little achievement of having eaten six steaks in six states in six nights on that wonderfully irresponsible trip that you and Norman Fox and I took.

As I look back, I see that our differences of attitude were seldom great and hardly ever enduring, though by nature you were the more liberal. By attrition we wore them down to mere grains or to nothing at all. Now, if I seem to quarrel with you on one point, I'm quarreling with myself, too. Maybe it's more accurate to say that I'm exposing, through you, a contradiction that exists within nearly every Montanan and grows sharper and sorer with time.

You used to say, quoting Thoreau, that you wanted a broad margin to your life. You even titled a book *Montana Margins* because here you found them wide. In the Montana State University magazine, *Venture*, you were quoted:

"This sums up what I want in life—room to swing my arms and to swing my mind. Where is there more opportunity than in Montana for creation of these broad margins, physical and intellectual? Where is there more opportunity to enjoy the elemental values of living, bright sun and clean air and space? We have room. We can be neighbors without getting in each other's hair. We can be individuals."

Amen.

But at the same time you always argued for resource development, for instance for the cheap power which would attract industry, which would create jobs. It was typical of you to want communities to prosper, to want people to enjoy opportunities. So, though you spoke in terms of small, home industry, weren't you really on both sides of the fence as most of us are today—margins on the one hand, masses on the other? Jobs mean people, and people restrict margins.

You ought to see us today. Everywhere is a wild proliferation of Americans. Nationally we have admitted thousands and thousands of European refugees, as perhaps we should. Both developments affect Montana, as do recent years of industrial expansion and at least moderate prosperity. Your home city of Great Falls is growing fast. So is Billings. So are other cities. So are little towns like Choteau. Even the canyon begins to seem crowded. It's a temptation to say that whereas we used to go there to get away, now we go there to get mobbed.

A man can't oppose growth, I guess. He can't be unconcerned about the needs of people. But he still can regret our shrinking margins, recognizing himself as a personality split beyond the guiles of all psychiatry.

That was you, Joe. And that's us.

Now, for readers, some words about your book. (The boon of television has come to Great Falls since you left.)

When Joseph Kinsey Howard died in August of 1951, I said that Montana had lost her conscience. Who but he could push and lead us to a recognition of our shortcomings? Who would tackle prejudice and privilege and so awaken us to them? What voice would speak for the neglected, the oppressed, the victimized? Or for our misused inheritance of soil and water and timber? Who would give vitality and direction to the sense of right? Who would see and set us straight?

No one, I thought, and I was wrong. Joe Howard still speaks and, speaking, exemplifies some lines he liked (from *The Doomsday Book*, by Edgar Lee Masters, Macmillan, 1920).

Take any life you choose and study it:
It gladdens, troubles, changes many lives.
The life goes out, how many things result?
Fate drops a stone, and to the utmost shores
The circles spread.

In 1943, when *Montana: High, Wide, and Handsome* appeared, its circles seemed, if not minute, at least confined. Confined, that is, to areas outside Montana. Elsewhere it sold immediately and well, but in Howard's home state, in the state it dealt with, it was often kept under bookstore counters if it was stocked at all. The reason was simple. The truth hurt.

Who was this Howard, anyhow, to criticize established ways, to delve and question and accuse? Let him go back to Canada where he was reared, or to Iowa where he was born! A left-wing pipsqueak of a Great Falls newspaperman, that's what he was, with no right to attack respected institutions, least of all the Anaconda Copper Company. Where would Montana be but for the Anaconda? And it was true—wasn't it?—that Howard was a leading fomenter of the Newspaper Guild.

Screwy Joe, his critics called him then. A Communist, they whispered, though he was as American as the high plains and the Bill of Rights. Communist? Really? Yes, they charged by implication at least, at a time when he was engaged in a community study supported by a national foundation. Those of us who knew him knew then that blood could boil. His accusers before the foundation, incidentally, came closer to losing their scalps than taking his.

It wasn't Anaconda alone that the book offended. It was its friends and business associates. It was some of the ranchers, who were not only sympathetic with the company but also confirmed in ways of land use that Howard decried. It was the complacent people. It was the people shaped in thought by old circumstances, the people of whom Howard spoke when he said of early get-rich-and-run behavior:

"It was an inauspicious beginning for a Treasure State, for thus was established a social and economic pattern of spoilation which subsequently was impressed upon the laws, customs, and even minds of Montanans and their eastern exploiters."

But not all people anywhere are prejudiced, and not all those with prejudices are out of reach of reason. Neither can suppression effectively suppress nor calumny convict. It took time in Montana for the book to be accepted, but it was accepted. It took time for it to be respected, but, except by diehards, it is respected. In any first-rate bookstore these days it is a standard item. It sells, though seventeen years have rolled by since its arrival. Most important, it had and continues to have an influence on Montanans of which more will be said.

This is a book about a lot of things, from the dried buffalo bones that littered the plains in the nineties to the Federal Reserve policy that dried the state up in the twenties. It is about John Wesley Powell, the prophet honored too late, whose ideas about the management of Western lands would have saved many a heartbreak. It is about the copper kings and their brazen capers in business and politics. It is about cattle and ranchers and rustlers. It is about Jim Hill's railroad and the poor rubes who were attracted by visions of gold ploughed out of ground which turned out to be richer in weeds. It is about Indians and the mistreatment of Indians. It is about taxes and tax fights, about water and water rights and the wasting of soil and the rain that was all the state (as well as hell) needed. It deals with past, present, and future, with geography and climate, with politics and economics and belated but promising planning. It concludes with a chapter, now seen as truly prophetic, in which is predicted a vast increase of commerce between Montana and the provinces of Canada along the old but new North Trail.

No one but a Montanan and no Montanan but Howard could have written this work. It is his, an expression of love and concern and knowledge told with rare skill. Additions, if anyone tried them, would be unseemly; attempts at detraction have failed. It stands by itself.

A quarrelsome book, the reader might conclude from what has been said here. Let us say courageous instead. Let us say good-natured, too, and humble and perceptive and eloquent with feeling for environment.

The sky is so big that the newcomers' mighty air transports roaring into the sunset will loom no larger than did the covered wagons creaking over a mountain pass. For an instant they will be noisy and important, and there will be a flick of flame on their wings, celestial tribute to gallantry; then the sky will be still again . . . save for the high chorus of color, which one learns to hear after a while.

The sunset holds infinite promise. Fire sweeps up from behind the Rockies to consume the universe, kindles the whole horizon, and all the great sky is flame; then suddenly it falters and fades atop the distant peaks and lonely buttes, ebbs and is lost in secret coulees. The Montanan is both humbled and exalted by this blazing glory filling his world, yet so quickly dead; he cannot but marvel that such a puny creature as he should be privileged to stand there unharmed, and watch.

What, then, are the assessable effects of *Montana: High, Wide, and Handsome,* assuming—which we can't—that it is the one and only factor in any alteration? Has it worked a revolution? Is the good earth treated better now? Has the pattern of spoilation changed? Is the Anaconda not the Anaconda any more?

Yes and no to the specifics. The revolution is rather an evolvement, and a slow one. Concern about soil has grown, though not enough. Spoilers seem fewer and less bold and certainly are more closely watched. The Anaconda deservedly is in better odor.

What Howard really has done is to encourage the spirit of Montanans, to lessen the suspicion of novelty, to promote a disposition to examine what has been sanctified. It is hardly too much to say that a public conscience has grown and is still growing out of his. Subjects are opener, individuals bolder, the mental climate more bracing. Even the executives of the Anaconda may tell you privately these days that the company's virtual monopoly of the daily press is bad business. In addition to all this, there have arisen a fresh interest in antecedents, a fresh appreciation of environment, a fresh concern with the future.

For all these advances major credit must go to Howard, who spoke and continues to speak in what is, simply, the best regional study written to date.

That's it, Joe.

As ever,
Bud

Here is an excerpt from A. B. Guthrie, Jr.'s introduction to American Odyssey: The Journey of Lewis and Clark, *a beautiful picture book edited and photographed by Ingvard Henry Eide and published in 1969 by Rand McNally & Company.*

AMERICAN
ODYSSEY

What a land [Lewis and Clark] saw! What an empire, stretching from the Falls of the Ohio or St. Louis— depending on your reckoning—to the misty mouth of the far Columbia! It stares at you, this country does, from old reports, made real, made here and now, by inadequate description. Inarticulation has its rightness and its eloquence. What say about a world known by no one save fractionally by aborigines? How get the feel of first-trod spaces? How express discovery? How bring home the awe of finding rivers never charted, much less named, of lifting eyes to mountains not imagined, of gazing dizzy over plains and prairies beyond the little measurements of woodsmen?

Lewis put laborious pen to paper after seeing the Great Falls of the Missouri and later on despaired:

> [A]fter wrighting this imperfect description I again viewed the falls and was so much disgusted with the imperfect idea which it conveyed of the scene that I determined to draw my pen across

it and begin agin, but then reflected that I could not perhaps suc-
ceed better than pening the first impression of the mind . . .

But his lines and those of Clark, misspelled, faltering, insufficient,
are yet eloquent when one trades his place for theirs. It was marvels made
them stumble. I have a word for the Expedition's responses to experience.
The word is "wonder," a wonder beautifully reflected by Clark's repeated
"butifull."

The wild Great Falls is in servitude now, a tame domestic of the Montana Power Company. Elsewhere the plow, the bulldozer, the town dump
and the irrigation ditch have changed and defaced the wonderland of
Lewis and Clark. But these liberties, regrettable if often warranted, are
minute by comparison with those taken by the Corps of Engineers and
the Bureau of Reclamation, hereafter called the Engineers, because—
cite what contributions to welfare you will—both are despoilers, both
the ready arms of the pork-barrelers in Washington. Neither one gives
a hoot about history or knows as much about ecology as your nearest
county agent.

On the great watershed of the Columbia their work has been done,
maybe. On the Missouri it hasn't. Between the headwaters of Fort Peck
Reservoir and Montana Power's Morony Dam there lie two hundred miles
of free-flowing water, of virtually virgin stream.

What a waste! What an opportunity for the Engineers' talents. So rich
was the promise that they came up with eleven proposals for development, only one of which contemplated no dams at all, though the National Park Service and other conservationists argued for a wilderness
waterway. After consultations and hearings the Engineers naturally decided in favor of dams, one at Fort Benton and one at High Cow Creek.
Described by that contradictory term, multipurpose, they would have
almost no purpose save the production of power. Though neither has
been authorized, both are being pushed, never fear, by the Engineers as
well as small-town boosters who would trade history permanently in
return for temporary hard cash. With the cash registers jingling, what
would it matter that many a visible and cherished association with national adventure and destiny washed lost beneath the waves?

Long before the present crop of Engineers was born, Mark Twain,
revisiting the Mississippi, commented on the work of the then-called
United States River Commission. His words apply to the Missouri and
other streams, as experience has demonstrated:

The military engineers of the commission have taken upon
their shoulders the job of making the Mississippi over again—a
job transcended in size by only the original job of creating it. . . .
One who knows the Mississippi will promptly aver—not aloud
but to himself—that ten thousand River Commissions with the
mines of the world at their back, cannot tame that lawless stream,
cannot curb it or confine it . . .cannot bar its path with an obstruc-
tion which it will not tear down, dance over and laugh at.

But I doubt they teach Mark Twain at the spawning grounds of
Engineers.

The stretch of stream between Fort Benton and the Fort Peck Reservoir gets especial attention here not only because it is in danger of destruction but also because it is pristine, pristine beyond the lingering nature
of any other reach of water ridden by the Expedition. Land passage, still
subject to some argument, has been determined, charted, and marked,
and its features have been celebrated by acknowledgment and enduring
name, though portages and foot passes in "butifull" valleys now play host
to carp and catfish. Along the dammed Missouri and along the dammed Columbia once-famous tributaries have been flooded, their mouths
pushed back, or have been dammed themselves. Landmarks await the
scuba diver.

But here. But here. Here in the Missouri's breaks and badlands, among
wonders ancient but made new by first enchantment.

Men besides me have made sure of camping sites and pitched camp
where the Expedition camped, have seen what Lewis and Clark saw and
have answered to it richly in poor words. And as it was, so is it yet. We
are the captains and the crew. They turn into us. All the marvels, all the
wonderments, are so much held in common that the beaver spanking
water with its tail is the very one that caught attention a century and
a half and more ago. A solitary cow becomes a buffalo.

If it appears from what I've said that no mark of historical importance
remains save on this little stretch of the Missouri, I have gone astray. There
are meadows yet and mountains, hollows and headlands, passes and pines
not yet devoured, landforms and foaming creeks: all identifiable, all
remindful of America's greatest journey.

Time will chip away at them, time and transmutation in the name
of progress, but they remain, lying or standing or streaming like fugitives
from the future; and the man who knows our history revives and rein-
carnates himself by seeing them.

In a personal letter dated December 5, 1986, Guthrie recalled that "a good many years ago, on Missoula's observance of Earth Day, I was asked to write a short piece [for The Sunday Missoulian, *April 18, 1971] dealing with the care of the planet. I doubt I will ever say it better or more concisely than I did then."*

Today, Guthrie recalls the writing of this brief essay—headlined by the paper "Earth Week 1971"—and the significant positive response it garnered, as the catalysts prompting a crusade that would consume a great deal of his time and energy in the years following.

A MESSAGE
TO THE YOUNG

The belief that the world was made for man, as the Scriptures have it, threatens to be the end of us. We have had our dominion over the fish of the sea, the birds of the heavens and over the cattle and every creeping thing, and we have been fruitful and multiplied, and we have subdued the earth, all as ordained; and the dread end looms as deprivation if indeed not extinction.

So long as we had a frontier with its seemingly limitless forests and fields, clear waters and metals there for the taking, the concept to many seemed tenable, even though keener eyes of decades ago already were discerning the ruin it would cause if unchecked.

Greed was at work, too, an assured and thoughtless greed hardly faced yet with the grim results of its grasping. As it was at work then, so it is at work now, more nakedly, though, and more egregiously because its aftereffects have become evident everywhere—evident in fouled air, poisoned streams, lakes dead or dying, in perished and perishing species and in the increase in physical, human disorders.

It is late, just maybe too late, to manage correction, but there is hope in the awakening consciousness and active endeavor of press and public and further hope in the growing awareness and outrage of young people.

I say to them: Be outraged! Too often you have dissented and protested without aim, or without an aim worthy of your outward expressions. But here is a cause. Embrace it, all of you! We oldsters will thank you, your generation will thank you, and future generations, if there be any, will be in your debt.

A. B. Guthrie, Jr. read the following essay as keynote speaker at the Montana Land Use Conference held in Billings on November 10, 1973. When he had finished, the applause was more than enthusiastic. Novelist Ken Kesey was the first among the large audience to come to his feet; within seconds Guthrie was receiving a unanimous standing ovation.

WEST IS
ANOTHER WORD
FOR MAGIC

I suppose I am an antiquarian. I value the past. I treasure what I know of it and prize what remains of it. Sometimes I remind myself of the man who had reached the century mark. A reporter, interviewing him, said, "You must have seen a lot of changes in your lifetime," to which the old man replied, "Yep. And I've been agin' 'em all!"

But in a sense, all Montanans are antiquarians. The paintings we admire, the paintings now being painted—most of them deal with our past. So it is with Montana literature, both fiction and nonfiction. Pictures and words hark back to the days of the fur hunter, the buffalo, the Indian and the cowpuncher. It is not mere curiosity that makes these subjects interesting: it is yearning for things that are vanished, for the old, free, less-fettered times, recoverable now only with paint and prose. With these aids we are taken back and, taken back, have the sad sense of having been born too late, into a dull time of steel and stone, of concrete and computer, of outdoor grills where once campfires burned.

Even as we hunger for those days, however, we go on destroying what remains of what made them, for all change means some destruction, all progress goodbye.

Begin with a small, even amusing example. The old-time cowpuncher, for lack of other entertainment, used to memorize the labels on tin cans, or "airtights," as they were called. He did, that is, if he could read.

When he wasn't doing that, maybe he played the mouth organ. "Red Wing" was one of the later favorites. Then came the circulation of magazines and books and still later radio and finally television, that mixed blessing.

Where, then, was the loss? What had progress shucked off? Ask as an answer what happened to the old-time storyteller. He had appeared out of the no-man's land of communication and entertainment. High in imagination, artful with words, clever in his effects, he was the sunshine and solace for lonely men who gathered in bunkhouse or camp to hear him. Some of these entertainers were skillful enough to give permanence to their stories through print, but not many.

The reference is to men like Charlie Russell and Will Rogers and yet another insufficiently recognized. His name was Con Price, and he lived in Montana, and he wrote two rich and wonderful books. They are *Trails I Rode* and *Memories of Old Montana*.

What happened to Con Price and the rest? Where are their successors? Nowhere, that's where. Progress took them away. They are lost, dead, aborted in the wash of radio and TV. We shan't see their likes again, nor shall we hear a song like Badger Clark's, who wrote, "How could such as they"—the "they" refers to settled eastern farmers plowing ancestral fields—"How could such as they understand the way we have loved you, young, young land?" And that is a loss.

A small loss, this extinction of the storyteller and the unabashed joy-singer of songs, but a loss nonetheless. A small loss in view of the greater gain, but still a sacrifice to change.

What of bigger losses? What has happened and is happening to us?

West is another word for magic. The West symbolizes adventure, freedom, space and gold, not only of troy weight but the gold of Eden. It is this magical symbolism which accounts for our hungering for vanished times, which accounts for our pictures and stories. Before ever we were a nation, long before, a Spanish explorer of the continent, bravely lost in the wilderness, wrote, "We always held it certain that, going toward the sunset, we should find what we desired."

Yet, for old-timers like me, some of that magic has gone with the years, dulled, lessened or lost through what we call progress. It is well to realize that progress leaves us no retreat. In Montana, in the entire West, much space has been fenced necessarily, and much has been subdivided, some necessarily, some without reason or forethought, and more space than can be easily measured has been sacrificed to the enthusiasm for highways. The conviction of the highwaymen—make it a pun if you choose—their conviction is that the straightest and fastest line between two points is the best, regardless of damage to drainage and nature, regardless of the pleasure of slower meanders through pleasanter country.

And let our rivers be dammed, in both senses of that word. Through the zeal of the Bureau of Reclamation and the Army Corps of Engineers, catfish and suckers now laze around the camping places of Lewis and Clark and the stopping points of the Astorians. Some of these dams appear necessary and justifiable, though silt will determine their real practicality, though effects unimagined at first already are prompting second thoughts, even among engineers. In a case or two or more, present dams have no excuse for being, except that during construction they kept engineers busy and added to the ringing of cash registers, sounding over the silent voices of history.

Our sod has been torn up, acres and acres that should have been left to the native grasses that buffalo and, later, cattle thrived on. Where, just where now, is the old buffalo grass? And even summer fallowing, that great and profitable answer to steady, dry-land cropping, is souring the land.

And what of adventure, Old Western style? The style commemorated by Charlie Russell in paint and Teddy Blue Abbott in prose? We in Montana are not in the full blush of what may be, but nightmares with some substance show the mountains noisy, crowded and scarred by motorized vehicles and adventures limited to the bagging of game made inedible by alien chemical intake, to the catching of a trout bred and reared artificially and, full of horse meat, planted tame just yesterday in a tainted stream or polluted lake.

As our water is tainted, so is our air, and the end is not yet. Hoerner-Waldorf wants to spend millions more on enlargement of its paper mill in Missoula County, though it can't meet or hasn't met the clean-air standards set by the state and so operates under an allowance for variance. So it is elsewhere, so it is everywhere. Industry, payrolls and profits, and to hell with the eventual effects on nature and man.

"Growth," we say. "Growth," the magic word, forgetting as we say it that growth, long continued, leads to decline and eventual death. "Size," we say, equating quantity with quality, confusing the two, making them one. Vachel Lindsay wrote:

Let not our town be large,
Remembering that little Athens was the muses' home.
That Oxford rules the heart of London still
And Florence gave the renaissance to Rome.

But size, but more industry, will broaden the tax base, we are told. How long will we put up with that old lie, implying as it does that taxes will be lower and public services better? Size *increases* the tax rate. Witness New York or Los Angeles or any of the great cities. Witness the taxes in congested states. And are the problems fewer there? Is life better, more fulfilling? Is the rate of crime less?

More than two centuries ago, Alexander Pope wrote, "To stay where you are is somewhat to advance." Good as that reflection is, perhaps more to the point are the words of Satchel Page, the old Negro baseball pitcher, who said—and I paraphrase—"Never look back, 'cause somethin' might be gainin' on you."

We don't have to look back. Something has caught up with us, and more somethings will unless, unlike Page, we do look back.

Discussions like this one inevitably lead to Montana's coal fields and strip-mining. The fields will be mined. Make no mistake about that. Reluctantly, as an antiquarian who nevertheless depends on indoor heat, electric power and internal combustion, I will admit that they must be.

But mined *how?* That is the question.

I speak with too little knowledge of recently enacted laws and consequent regulatory agencies. Forgive me, then, if I approach the subject as if nothing had been done, as if now, and for the first time, we were tackling the problem. Here would be my suggestions:

Leave the matter not to the great companies. Pay no undue heed to their arguments. Pay no heed at all to their promises, for they're likely to be observed in the breach. Remember at all times that company spokesmen speak from the purse. When they talk about the general benefit, keep in mind who benefits first. When they speak about reclamation, recall how they've fought our efforts for a cleaner and better environment.

I am a conservative who believes in our system no matter the violence done it, and so I don't speak contemptuously of these spokesmen. They are doing their job as they see it, as perhaps they must if we believe that right answers come out of conflict. But the years have taught me how readily man is seduced. I know how easily any of us may be. We lean, all of us, to the side of self-interest, ignoring in doing so that we may lose our souls.

And remember that all of us are influenced, if unknowingly, by Scripture and by the frontier. The earth was made for man, the Bible would have us believe. Other creatures exist, if they continue to exist, by our sufferance. Edible, they are gifts from heaven. Pests, they defy explanation, except that they may be heaven's challenge to man. In any case they have no purpose unless they serve us. That is the long-time ethic.

And here, sure enough, in our developing years as a nation, was a new world made for man, a world rich beyond belief, a world of endless opportunity and promise. So we mined the land, felled the timber and dug the metals, all with extravagance, knowing that over the next hill were virgin acres, stands of timber and likely strikes. And so it was that we pillaged a continent and thrived in the process, forgetting that earth is exhaustible. No, not forgetting it; being dead sure it wasn't.

Something of that feeling is in us still, no matter that, to paraphrase Page again, somethin' has caught up with us. That attitude and the residual feeling that a man has a right to do what he will with what he owns. By extension, until lately, that individual right was the corporate right.

It was out of good intention, out of buoyant confidence, that we allowed things to happen. Most of us have not been willing accomplices to assault on the earth. We just didn't think. We might remind ourselves that good and thoughtless intentions work badly in practice.

What to do, then, about strip-mining?

Since the coal will be dug, let us set up every safeguard, guided not by commercial interests but by reason and our love for the land we have so often betrayed. Let government set the standards. Let it enact laws with teeth, directed by dispassionate and informed minds. Let it make sure about reclamation. Let it safeguard our waters.

Worry not, for even the strictest laws will not discourage development. Industry howls about the impossible and, forced to, then does it— an accomplishment much to its credit. Let us engrave on our minds that our first concern must be water, soil and air. We can't stay progress, but we can guide it. As we do so we should reflect that every choice entails an onus, that every decision leaves the residue of regret, that the path ahead leaves behind something dear.

Since we can't see clearly what is ahead, let us approach our future gently, with careful regard for what it may be.

Soren Kierkegaard, the Danish philosopher, said more than a hundred years ago: "He who fights the future has a dangerous enemy. The future is not, it borrows its strength from the man himself, and when it has tricked him out of it, it appears outside of him as the enemy he must meet."

Please, not anymore, let us make an enemy of the future.

This essay is excerpted from the text of a talk A. B. Guthrie, Jr. delivered on January 17, 1974, to the annual banquet of the Bozeman, Montana Chamber of Commerce. Here is an example of Guthrie's open-minded good humor and willingness to speak his convictions—even in the face of an almost certainly unsympathetic audience.

A VOICE
OF ANGER
AND THUNDER

I am an odd selection to speak at a chamber of commerce meeting, for—though I recognize, with sympathy, some of the problems businessmen face today—I can't be uncritical.

Local organizations like yours vocally fight shy of politics, though the rude fact remains that you are in it. Commerce and politics are inseparable, no matter the veils drawn on participation.

And big business is up to its ears in politics. Witness the great and shady contributions to presidential elections. Witness ITT. Witness the dairy industry. Witness the present energy shortage, which we can't be sure is an actual shortage or one contrived by business through government.

These involvements are beyond your correction, perhaps beyond any correction, but if I were you, I would be sore. For these mammoth manipulations, covert or open, put a bad face on all business, including yours. And, with unknown exceptions, you don't deserve it.

Not that chambers of commerce always distinguish themselves in their concern for the general welfare. The Missoula chamber has endorsed a massive enlargement of the Hoerner-Waldorf paper mill, though the plant has yet to meet the state's clean-air standards. The Missoula chamber in fact voted for the cash register and greatly increased pollution as against the general health, as against the not-insignificant matter of nuisance. I call that stand antisocial.

Just recently, the athletic council of the Missoula chamber staged a girlie party, which I understand included choice movies and gambling. I look with a high degree of indifference on such antics, allowing for the nature of sport-loving men and the possibility that some of their absent wives may be nature's revenge on the peeping Tom. But many people are not so tolerant. Many regard the party as a sin and a shame and a threat to the moral fiber of a community which, in presumably cleaner days, nevertheless produced the party-goers.

The corollary is that, perhaps, these dirty days will produce decency tomorrow.

Ever since her earliest days as territory and state, Montana has endured colonial status as supplier to the outside. Her trees have been felled for interests far away. Her minerals have been mined for distant uses. Her coal has been coveted by strangers. And as it was, so is it.

The world must live, the promoters say, omitting the idea that Montana's own life is at stake.

Montana, the land of shining mountains, of high plains, of grandeur unsurpassed, of felt, free adventure, of a way of life grown almost unique. A mindless progress decrees that she must go.

You look at the evidence, and you cry out in grief, in dismay and in outrage, and your voice is lost to the winds of money and greed. It is a whisper in the mad clatter of coin and machinery. It is a murmur—if ever noticed—in the clamor for Montana's diminished and diminishing capital.

Where is the voice of Montana? Whose is the voice? Where is the far-heard voice of fact, of prescience, of anger and thunder? Who can command heed?

I listen for that voice.

Guthrie wrote this essay on October 15, 1974, as a script to accompany a slide presentation concerning Montana land use.

LAND:

USE AND

ABUSE

am A. B. Guthrie. Because it is my professional name and too much trouble to change, I tack a "Junior" onto it, though my father has been dead for years. I make my living by writing, mostly about the West, often about Montana, a state I choose to live in because I love it.

Often we need to be reminded of our blessings. With a fresh eye and renewed appreciation we need to see the great roll of our plains, the majesty of our mountains, the beauty of our valleys. All of it—every fruitful field, every stretch of grazing land, every spire, every forest, every far horizon—is a wonder. What places offer more? What places as much?

Though my work is indoors these days, it was not always so. I have worked in field and forest, with livestock, with horses and the machines that replaced them. I have been around for a long time, longer than most of you, and I keep rejoicing at the beauties of a state in which I have spent a large part of my life.

Though in per-capita income we are far from the richest state in the union, we have riches not to be measured. We have a good way of life in Montana, a way more free and open than most people are granted. We have fish in many untainted streams. On plains and in mountains elk and antelope graze and deer browse. Ducks inhabit our bodies of water. Grouse of numerous kinds live in lowland and upland. Beyond these riches, though part and parcel of them, most important though related, we can count the possession of space, space to live life in. We live in grandeur.

These advantages, plus residual natural resources, are becoming known to outsiders who not so long ago regarded Montana as a poor and frostbitten outland. Hundreds, even thousands of them, wanting, as they say, to get away from it all, have come or plan to come or want to come to the state. By coming, they bring or will bring it all with them. They travel with what they seek to escape, to their disappointment and our disadvantage.

And outside money has disvovered that there's gold in them thar hills, gold in the form of coal under hill and field, gold in real-estate speculation, gold in supermarkets and subdivisions.

It is sad that these invaders get help from some Montanans themselves.

As I look back and ahead, I wonder what we are doing to ourselves, what we are allowing to be done to us. Not only to us but to our children and our children's children and succeeding generations of man. What of our soil? What of our timber? What of our water? What of our air? Where goes our prized space?

Such is our tradition that frontier beliefs cling to us. Much can be said in their favor. They support our independence. They emphasize individuality. They have kept us, as a nation, from falling into the trap of dictatorship, either right-wing or left. They are part of the rights of free men.

The question is: How far do the rights of ownership go?

Let's start with an example of what we are letting be done, though individual or corporate ownership is not involved here. A drive through the Bitterroot country will show even the most casual observer what unwise logging can do and has done. You see the sides of mountains clearcut. You see the erosion that follows in the wake of the tractor. You can see in too many places how forlorn are the prospects of reforestation. By these glimpses you can imagine the damage done to the watershed. You can count on faster spring run-offs and shrunken summer flow as a result.

Of course we need timber, lumber for new houses, for industrial installations, for government buildings, for other uses unmentioned. We must have it and we can, without the damage seen here. Selective cutting is the answer. Visit a forest that a skilled and dedicated forester has managed, and you'll find the old delights undiminished. You'll hardly be aware that any cutting has been done at all.

For the damage done in the Bitterroot we may blame companies. We may lay it to national policy. But first of all we must blame ourselves. We allowed it to happen. By what right? With what thought? With what regard for the future?

We come to soil and strip-mining. Here was once agricultural land. Here grasses and crops grew and cattle grazed. Will they ever again? Will they after vast acreages as yet untouched by machine have been gouged and up-ended? We can hope so, but we cannot be sure, no matter that reclamation is promised. If the coal must be mined, as I fear it must, let's try to make sure that what follows is not disaster. Let's establish and enforce safeguards if we can. Let's not let the region become Appalachia. Assuming the worst, we may ask ourselves if companies have the right to do as they're doing. The right to leave that part of Montana a wasteland? To grab for and get allowances for the Yellowstone's flow and make the river a virtually dry channel below?

Does national emergency justify such a risk? A sour note sounds here. Had it not been for last-minute interference by government, Montana's coal would have been tried out in Japan and, if shown suitable, shipped there by the thousands of tons.

I recognize the energy emergency. I understand the necessity of foreign trade. But I fear for Montana. I fear she'll pay dear. I fear she'll be made to destroy a good part of herself, as she surely will unless we take every precaution.

Not that the coal miners are alone in their abuse of the land. Consider the fact that wild and nutritious grasses grew stirrup-high in days that old-timers remember. Try to find such growth now and then wonder about overgrazing. Look at fields once plowed and abandoned and left to grow up in tumbleweed and Russian and Canadian thistle.

Put your mind to the unscrupulous and ubiquitous subdivider who takes productive land out of production, encroaches on the domain of wildlife and gives purchasers a poor bargain to boot. Think of sprawling shopping centers that not only appropriate space but also spell the death of downtowns, as in Great Falls, as in Missoula, as elsewhere. Not good, I say, without knowing what we can do. Here is a vexed matter of rights, to be determined, if ever it is, by public authorities with help from the public.

Easier to approach is the subject of atmosphere. Through ownership of a site is it the right of a company, or a man for that matter, to poison the air above and beyond and far from the seat of operations? The air that all of us breathe? Should a company be free to function when fumes from factory and stack kill outside vegetation, stunt and deform livestock and wildlife and so do sure damage to humans that only time will determine? These questions answer themselves.

Many of you will remember streams that ran full, clear and pure, as you will remember times when you could not only catch fish and shoot birds but eat their flesh without fear. What has happened to those streams and those times? What poisons do our shrunken waters carry? Waste from factories for one thing. Sewage from cities and towns for another. And—let's admit it though it poses a sore problem—drainage from fields treated with herbicides and pesticides.

Over in the Couer d'Alene [Idaho] country it has just been discovered that children who drank water polluted by industry suffer from lead poisoning. And here in Montana we have a recent case of wrong and hazardous practice. On the lower Teton River a hog-waste lagoon washed out. For miles that waste killed all the fish. I don't know what it did or may do to livestock. I don't know what it may do to wells and thus to riverside dwellers. Only time can tell. But the question is immediate: Was it the right of those who made and used the lagoon to do as they did, to take chances, to operate with careless disregard for the health of the stream and the creatures and people below? Is it any owner's right to do so?

I want Montanans to be healthy and happy. Many of us are. We are even in the face of unhappy changes, in the face of other, even unhappier changes that may be. Insofar as I believe in progress, I believe in orderly and prudent development, with due regard for those who come after us.

Even yet we can save Montana. We can keep Montana Montana. As individuals and as individuals acting in groups we can do it. Through the agencies of government expressing our will we can do it, though doing it may require a new view of selfish and individual rights as opposed to the larger yet individual need. We can promote health and happiness and prosperity itself if we are bold enough to forward the measures now called for.

The conflict between freedom and necessity confronts us. A philosopher said—and I believe the quotation says it all—"Freedom is the recognition of necessity."

Guthrie read the following essay at the Woodside Grange Hall in Hamilton, Montana, on December 5, 1974. His audience was a gathering of The League of Women Voters and like-minded citizens.

BETTER
TO CALL IT
CHANGE

I am glad to be here, to appear before this unit of the League of Women Voters.

Without partisanship, the League stands for principles not always popular. It brings intelligence to human problems. More than that, it brings influence. It is active and effective in the push of ideas. It merits pride in itself and thanks from outsiders.

Not until Mr. Brandborg, a member himself, told me last spring did I know that the League is open to men. That's rather a switch from the present insistence that domains traditionally exclusive to men be opened to women. I support that insistence, being half a women's-libber myself. I could be more than that if it didn't appear from the pictures I've seen and the declarations I've read that true-blue women's-libbers hate men one and all.

For the sake of recruitment I could wish that your name were different. It's too late for that, I suppose. But I suspect that a lot of men in their male pride will think twice about it, will hesitate to join any congregation of women so-called—unless, of course, it's a harem.

It is doubtful that I'll say anything tonight that this group won't tend to agree with. It's almost never that I'm invited to speak before hostile audiences. So you may go home saying I've merely repeated what you already knew, the same old thing. That's a trouble with causes and the supporters of causes. We get tired of our own thoughts and words. We become fagged out and indifferent—which the opposition never does.

But if there is disagreement, let it be considered disagreement, not blind and offended objection. It is not my purpose to excite anger or to arouse controversy, but, rather, if I can, to encourage thought.

Recently, a scientist wrote that it had taken him five years to reverse an opinion once strongly held. Equating himself, then, with the run of mankind, whom he considered no brighter or duller than he, he put the average for a change of mind at five years. That seems a long time for the percolation of a good idea—and his was good. Wrong ones seem to brew faster.

As a further introduction let me say that I'm independent, with no ties to party, corporations or pressure groups. But in my small individual way, I do have an axe to grind. The axe is the future of Montana and, by extension, all peoples.

The subject tonight is conservation. It is land use and abuse. It is pure water and poisoned. It is clean air and dirty. And it is something more. It's too bad there's no room for humor here. In the face of serious illness, one doesn't make jokes.

We'll start at home. This county [Ravalli] and town are familiar with Forest Service policy and logging practice. Most of you probably have seen areas of clear-cut in neighboring forests. You may have deplored them or merely suffered them or even endorsed them. I think a forward look, a look into the future, demands that we fight past and present Forest Service policy and practice down to the last ditch.

Consider:

How long does it take for a tree to grow to respectable size, to maturity? Most of us will be lucky if we live that many years more.

Reforestation? How bleak the prospects appear when you scan the naked hillsides. How bleak when you know how few seedlings grow and thrive out of the thousands deposited. Can you ever expect to see such fine forests again in these denuded areas, forests like some that survive still, thanks to prudent management or difficult access?

Stream flow? Everybody knows, though few take heed, that flow is measured and meted by vegetation, by ground cover. Lay bare the hillsides, and you get erosion and rapid run-off and floods, followed by little or no flow at all. Some early spring day, examine the clear-cut land. You will see it lying naked, lying dry, though on the perimeter, under the sheltering canopy of trees left standing, the winter's snow still will lie.

Need I speak of the resulting pollution of rivers and streams, of silted and dirty water and the damage done, being done and yet to be done? No. You must be already aware of it.

Here, in this area, in all of western Montana, we face the question of jobs, of unemployment, of a general sickness in the economy. The problem is far more than local, but local circumstances are in point tonight. I have a great sympathy for gut hunger, none for pocketbook greed. As much as the most sympathetic of you, I want people to have jobs and wages and shelter and food. Massive logging is a poor and short-term way of assuring these necessities.

What, then? Well, then, perhaps a great federal program of repairing what we have wrought. A concerted effort toward a restitution to nature. I can see long work there and many jobs if the debt to earth is paid back.

Beyond the immediate, we must think of the consequences of continued wrong practice. Keep up extravagant logging, and you run out of logs. The sawyer saws himself out of a job. And what remains for his children and his children's children and the succession of men? No wood to cut. No jobs. Perhaps even no country worth living in.

Some years back I passed through Priest Lake, Idaho. It had been quite a town once. It wasn't when I saw it. It was a few human relics in a waste of stumps.

I am coming to another subject, coming roundabout. Years ago, long before the energy crises, I heard an aged and retired university president worrying about how long the world's oil would last. Later, in conversation with others, I laughed and asked why, at his age, he should worry. He wouldn't last as long as the oil.

I blush when I think about me in those days. A slob, a dumb kid smarting off. What did I care then, why should anyone care, about events after death?

Now I care. I care immensely. That's why I'm here. I think of posterity. I want a decent world left behind me. Thomas Jefferson once swore eternal enmity against any tyranny over the mind of men. I have sworn opposition to abusers of land.

Now let's leave western Montana and go east to the plains country. Observe those monsters of mining machinery gouging the land deep, raping acre on acre for the reward of coal. Seeing, you will ask: How much, how long, O Lord? Must we tear up and tear up our croplands and grasslands for fuel the world needs? Must we become the Appalachia I have seen in Kentucky? Will even a subsistence living be left after operators have tumbled the land and poisoned the waters?

Restoration, they say. Reclamation, they promise, after the coal in one section is gone and the greedy shovels move on. Promises. I wonder, I doubt. I have seen no evidence that native grasses, the grasses that nourished buffalo and, later, longhorns, and still later, Herefords, can be seeded successfully on ravished acres.

An added worry: If companies are allowed their way, what will become of the Yellowstone River? Will it be a poisoned trickle of water, a dry bed below operations? We don't know. All we know is that industrial demands for water threaten the life of the river.

In one way or another all of us have been nature's offenders. The cars we drive subject us to a toxic effluvium. The gadgets we buy involve waste. The containers and packages, demanded by us or foisted on us, are costly, and not just to the pocketbook. The factories we have permitted now dull the sun and punish our lungs. The stink and fallout from the Hoerner-Waldorf paper mill is not just a nuisance. It is a disgrace and an injury. We kill birds with pesticides. We kill fish. We kill game. What sportsman knows these days whether the trout he catches or the deer he shoots is fit to eat. Does the flesh contain mercury? Is it full of DDT? Has it been altered and made lethal by atomic dust from the heavens? Best be careful. The long chain of life includes man himself. Tinker with one link, and you tinker with all.

Some have contended that I stand against progress. That depends. I don't like subdividers except for the careful and few. I patronize shopping centers with a feeling of guilt, mourning the deaths of downtowns. I dispute the man who contends that his ownership of land gives him the right to do with it as he will, for no one really owns land. He serves as trustee. His term is limited, and it behooves him to leave his holdings undamaged, and undamaging to his neighbor's premises. As an old Indian said at the time of the Riel Rebellion, "We borrow this earth from God."

I can't stand against progress because I don't know what progress is. Neither does anyone else. Better to call it change, and change, though it may jingle the cash register, is no good if it comes at the cost of old and real values. One of our prime values is space. I don't want it destroyed by an influx of outsiders. Neither do I want greedy outside money investing in what it calls the development of Montana. We have enough people already, and development is a word for invasion and pay-off.

When our infant nation purchased the Louisiana Territory, Thomas Jefferson wanted families to occupy it. The land west was unlimited. Stake a claim, you and you, and bear families to stake claims. The world was ours and open and free and vast beyond measure.

With enthusiasm, with young buoyancy, with faith, without evil intent, we did just what he wanted. We occupied the land and produced sons and daughters to occupy more of it. We felled the forests, for the supply was beyond calculation. We mined the ore; there was plenty of it and plenty more to be found. We built mills and factories and founded cities and towns, for growth was the way of life, growth in numbers and activities and production and money. Bigger meant better, and bigger yet meant better yet. The notion of growth was in our bones. It was in our hearts and minds. And as it was, so it tends to be still.

Today I wish I could see Thomas Jefferson. I wish he could see us— that man who thought 10 people per square mile about the right limit of human congestion.

I have circled around the crux of the problem. I have spoken of effects, not the cause. I have dealt with symptoms, not their origin. The brute fact is that there are too many people on earth and still more on the way to being.

As I've mentioned, in our beginnings as a continental nation and up until too-recent times, big families were the rule. Indeed, they seemed to make sense in earlier years, since settlers needed the help of sons and daughters, and opportunity and land were unlimited. So we multiplied our kind, ignoring or laughing at what Malthus had said long, long before—that by geometrical increase man would cumber the earth, eventually to be reduced in number only by famine, pestilence and war.

Influenced by tradition, we continued, and some still continue, to breed big families, long after any justification has vanished. I speak with some authority here and a great deal of hurt, for I come from a family of nine and suspect that my mother would not have died when she did had she not been worn out with childbearing. A part of me died when she died. Never again would life be the same.

On a note of triumph someone may ask: How would I like it if I hadn't been born? The answer is simple: I would have been spared a great deal of trouble.

I am arguing for birth control, of course, for family limitation, and, in connection with these, abortion on request during the first trimester at least. To me it is ironic and wrong that men, some celibate, have had and still have so much say on the question of abortion. It's damn little of their business. Let the women decide. Let the individual women decide. It's not abortion as against no abortion. It's abortion as against enforced pregnancy and the unwanted child.

Thousands are starving in Asia and Africa and elsewhere, and we lay their sufferings and deaths to climate and crop failure, or unsettled economics and underdevelopment. These are factors, but the first factor of all is that they've been too prolific. In our humanity we try to feed them, ignoring the cruel likelihood that, by nourishing them, we increase their fertility.

In protest against limitation of families, it has been argued that birth control is a form of genocide. The Pope recently said that birth control in the famishing countries would take from the poor the pleasure of having children. Had he consulted the poor, I wonder? Did he have a consensus from the wives of the poor? Would he impoverish us all to support the poor and prolific? He didn't say. What did he know about the pleasure of having children? These questions are legitimate. They are mine to ask honestly, without irreverence.

The Pope didn't say, either, that the poor breed more children than those better off. Neither did he mention their much greater rate of infant mortality.

He might consider in his concern for the poor a fanciful suggestion made by the scientist I mentioned earlier: Put severe limits on family size among the poor, but let the rich breed away. In time, by that process, the poor would become the rich and the rich become the poor.

Only by recognizing that our planet has limited resources and can support only so many people do we get to the root of the problem. It must have occurred to you that man is a parasite. He feeds on Mother Earth. And some of you must have had the uneasy thought that he's killing his host. In order to save her and himself, he may finally have to resort to the extreme of compulsory limitation on births, abhorrent as that idea is to a free people.

You may ask what this general view has to do with Montana. It has a great deal to do with us. It bears on our situation. Why do Californians want to come here? Why do people from the East and Midwest and elsewhere? Because they're crowded where they are, that's why. They would answer that they want to get away from it all, the all created by human numbers and the proliferation of things. They want space. They want the freedom of space. They want a sequestered place on the banks of a good trout stream. That's what they want, and that's what they won't get if they come as they'd like to. That would be the end of us, the end of the Montana we know.

We can't raise a solid wall against immigration, of course, but by zoning and planning and careful restriction, we can guide and control our own growth. We can act against haphazard development.

I love Montana. She is home to me. She is my point of outlook on the universe. I have known her for a long time, and I have fished her streams and hunted her fields and ridden her trails and rejoiced in her majesty. And always, as John Burroughs said of his world, always have beauty and joy attended my coming and goings.

I look west from my place, and the mountains are mine, as they are everyone's who has eyes to see. I no longer hunt, but the sight of a deer heartens me. I make friends with the blue grouse that visit my highland cabin. The great roll of distance delights my sight. I welcome the warm wind, the chinook, and welcome the daily hour of no wind, when not even aspen leaves stir.

She is a mighty and wonderful world, our Montana, and I pray against the forces that would destroy her.

A. B. Guthrie, Jr. spoke these words on December 13, 1974, at the Symposium on Environmental Reporting held at the University of Montana, Missoula.

THE
RESPONSIBILITY
OF THE PRESS

f I am correctly informed, you are all newspaper people or free-lancers. As men with short experience in newspapermaking like to say, I used to be in the game. My time wasn't short, though. For more than 20 years I worked on a daily paper with a circulation of about 25,000, rising eventually to the exalted position of executive editor. Sometimes I could weep over my sins.

Twenty-five years and more later, my respect for good newspapers has risen—along with my anger that many papers neglect or ignore their responsibilities.

Freedom of the press, that often-abused right, does impose responsibilities. It involves the obligation to report fairly, to recognize the perils of advocacy in politics, to examine, to investigate, to fully and honestly inform the people whom the press serves. Unless it meets its duties, the press may lose its freedom.

During the Watergate investigation, I was yelling hurrah for the free press. I still say hurrah but am somewhat muted. Had it not been for just a couple of able and determined reporters, had it not been for one courageous publisher, Richard Nixon, I fear, would still be our president. I know that other papers and magazines joined and aided the investigation, but, so far as I know, they were followers of the *Washington Post* and *Newsweek*. To those two, particularly the *Post*, goes the first credit. To the rest, in the beginning at least, freedom of the press meant freedom not to make waves. That kind of freedom may spell its own doom.

The Watergate mess probably involved none of you, so consider yourselves outside my criticism there. Whether the rest of what I have to say bears upon you is for you to decide.

My subject is the environment, particularly the environment of Montana. Some of you, maybe all of you, know more about it than I, but none of you has stouter convictions.

Before I go on, I'd like to give a couple of pieces of advice. Pay no great heed to chambers of commerce. They're often wrong and their aims always short-term. Be chary of corporations and their spokesmen. On the surface, they'll always make a good case. I said on the surface. I would like to tell publishers to beware of that seduction called goodwill. Old Robert Scripps once said he could protect himself against his enemies, but God save him from his friends. You could call *The Missoulian* a controversial paper, yet in Davenport, Iowa, last summer, a Lee Enterprise authority told me that *The Missoulian* was one of the most flourishing newspapers in the chain.

So much for goodwill.

You don't have to travel far in Montana to see evidence of waste and despoliation, to observe how little attention developers pay to the consequences of their endeavors.

Everywhere you see supermarkets and subdivisions. You see the deaths of central cities and the appropriation of land once productive. The 93 Strip in Missoula is a disgrace. So is Ten Avenue South in Great Falls. Elsewhere the same thing is happening, even in small towns. What is Main Street anymore but a way to get somewhere else, to markets and eating places and bars and suburban homes.

And beyond our cities, I have visited the areas of clear-cut and been outraged. Will ever forests grow there again? Not in my lifetime or yours. Will rivers flow as they once did, naturally measured and metered by vegetation? Perhaps. Perhaps in some distant future that your children or grandchildren will be privileged to enjoy if we work hard and long at restoration and call a halt to destructive practices.

Across the mountains, there's strip-mining. Strip-mining. It is a compound word for compounded ruin. That land, gouged and tumbled and violated, won't and can't be reclaimed, no matter the promises. It was estimated optimistically years ago that ground overgrazed into deserts or needlessly plowed or cut over required half a century to recover. How much longer for earth that's been strip-mined?

These abuses are just a few of many. Don't ignore water. It is almost sure to be poisoned by strip-mining, as elsewhere it is poisoned by erosion, herbicides and pesticides. What will become of the Yellowstone River? Will it someday be a toxic trickle of water, a dry bed below operations? We don't know. We can only surmise. It is certain, though, the industrial demands for water threaten the life of the river.

In a sense, we have all been trapped by history, geography and tradition. All of us have. Not just Montanans. Our forefathers who settled this land had biblical assurance that earth was made for man. Let him do what he would with it then. The entire Louisiana Territory was open and unoccupied and waiting for development. Open and unoccupied, that is, except for the Indian, who was given short shrift. We would make a Christian and a farmer of him. The poor Indian didn't even have sense enough to know about individual property rights. We could put the land to a lot better use than he did.

Oh, sure.

So we settled the empty land and eventually built cities and towns, for growth was the way of life, growth in numbers and activities and production and money. The notion of growth was in our bones. It was in our hearts and minds. And as it was, so it tends to be still.

Newspapers have been among the leaders of this foolish parade. They have boosted their towns. They've endorsed efforts for factories and payrolls and what is falsely and euphemistically called an increase in the tax base. Now some papers are beginning to wonder and question.

How long will we continue to equate quantity with quality? How long will we think growth is strength? Cancers grow, too. The music of the cash register can be a requiem.

A book recently published is called *Topsoil and Civilization*. It lays the decay of once-great civilizations—those along the Nile, the Euphrates and the Mediterranean—it lays their decline and decay to the waste of topsoil. The soil disappeared because of ignorance, indifference, greed and wrong practice. So long as rich topsoil lay in those regions, so long could they support vigorous life. Wars might destroy one regime but another civilization rose if the fields were fruitful. When they ceased to be, the great empires went down.

Only briefly and, I think, with too little emphasis, does the book take into account the factor of man in his increasing numbers.

That's a subject I want to bring up, and it is touchy. The undeniable fact is that there are too many people on earth. As our health increases, as infant mortality is reduced, as the life span is extended, so are our numbers increased, and so is our distress.

By and large, the press hasn't tackled this problem, though it does report the conclusions and warnings given by researchers. I'm not sure that the time is right for editorial position. By ill-timing, the press might diminish its influence in the protection and preservation of the environment. But soon, if not quite yet, it must, as we say, bite the bullet.

That bullet is birth control.

A good many years ago I was asked to speak before a national meeting of the Food for Peace people. I told them they wouldn't want me, because I'd insist that any gift of food be accompanied by the gift of contraceptives and birth-control information. They didn't want me.

Our own laws promote procreation with their special allowances for the presence of children. Aid for Dependent Children, noble in motive as it is, encourages bastardy.

The whole subject of the conservation and preservation of the environment is abhorrent to the pioneer ethic. That ethic, in some respects right, it seems to me, emphasizes the independence of the individual and the rights of property. What real rights does the owner of a piece of land have? Is it his to do with as he will, regardless of damage to others? To posterity? Some owners still think so, ignoring the fact that they are mere trustees, appointed by providence to a limited term. With equal reasons, I believe, it can be asked whether a couple has the right to unlimited reproduction, thus reducing the space and resources available to others.

I haven't meant to diminish the environmental role of the press, no matter that it seems hardly ready to confront the fundamental problem. I am heart and soul in sympathy with the efforts of many papers and their reporters and editors.

I bless all of you who strive for decent surroundings, for old and real values that reckless progress would erase.

On October 25, 1975, A. B. Guthrie, Jr. presented the following to the Helena Historical Conference.

RETREAT
INTO LIMBO

In my newspaper days, a reporter asked a Greek restaurant owner if he were a native of Lexington, Kentucky.

"Sure," the owner replied. "I been a native for 17 years."

If you ignore the first six months of my life, I am a native Montanan.

I have been around for a long time. I have had opportunity to observe, to compare, to assess and just perhaps to foresee. Age may not make a man wise, but seven decades of experience give him advantages.

Youth inclines to think that the world around it has always been as it is. The young person is likely to accept, even to welcome, what is called progress, being ignorant of what change has done. Not all young people, mind you. The present concern with environment, the realization of waste, owe much to the awareness of youth. But not all youth, not youth by-and-large. Even to older people, change has come about so gradually that the present seems little altered from yesterday. It is not until age begins to cast back, to remember what was as against what is, that doubts and regrets and degrees of nostalgia set in, that the bright face of change starts to lose luster.

So it is with me. I am not fixed in opposition to all change. The conditions of life leave vast room for improvement. But change, proposed change, man-managed change, needs consideration, not haste. Blind change leaves sores and regrets, no matter that it marches under the colorful banner of progress.

In our early days, acting in an innocence later to be deplored, the fur hunters plundered our streams until hardly a beaver was left. Gone with the beaver was the life these men loved and destroyed by their profligacy. Then came the buffalo hunters, the hide hunters and after them the bone-pickers—for all that remained of the great herds was bone.

Almost at the same time, as well as afterwards, the streams along with their shores were again plundered, this time for gold. Hardly a grain of it remained after the panners and dredgers had finished their work.

Mining men found the richest hill on earth, and they and their successors gouged out the copper, and high old times came to Butte. Where is the copper now, where the high old times?

There were trees to be felled, too, great forests awaiting the saw. The saw wasn't long in coming, or the trees long in going. Now such is our condition that lumbermen hunger for the stands preserved on the public domain, and of late years the Forest Service, relaxing its role as conserver, has been sympathetic.

It becomes tedious to tell what you already know. The fact to be kept in mind, though, to be kept first in mind, is that we in Montana have invaded the gifts we inherited. We have drawn on our principal. We have lived off it. We have sold off, we are still selling off what can't be replaced and in the process are leaving behind us destruction that can't be assessed in full yet.

Much of the exploitation, much of unthinking damage was done in innocence, in innocent exuberance, in a spirit characteristic of pioneer America. Growth was the way of life. It was the nature of things. And here, before American eyes, was a whole continent of riches, riches beyond measure. The end was not yet. The end never would be. That's what we thought.

We know better now. At least we are beginning to know better, though not to all men does the knowing impose any restraint. There are too many among us who think first and only of the immediate personal profit, not of the long-term and irreparable loss. They figure to hell with it. Others, really well-meaning others, rationalize their behavior, telling themselves they are satisfying a public need—to their advantage, of course. I see that kind of self-deception working in the effort to enlarge the number of power stations at Colstrip.

Study the balance sheet. Except for coal, we are virtually out of minerals. Even Butte, that once-thriving city, is moribund. We are shy on timber. Forests have been so thinned, so abused by clear-cutting, that years are necessary for reclamation, and then only if we arrive at prudent practice. Streams ran foul that once ran pure. Spring floods, the holding cover of vegetation gone from the headwaters, visit us, and then water courses dry up. Land, much marginal land, has been plowed. Forsaken, as many acres have been, it becomes host to weeds. Other acres, untouched by the plow, have been grazed to the last stem and will be grazed again when spring brings hope to the plains. Where, these days, can one find that nutritious native of the prairies, buffalo grass?

The old riches gone or largely gone, we have turned to and begun marketing the greatest value of all. That value is space.

Montana, the land of limitless space—just as the forests and deposits of minerals and prime farming land once were thought to be without limits. Outlanders—jammed elbow-to-elbow in their concrete canyons, stifled in their homes by neighbors equally stifled, harried and irritated by traffic on their ways to and from work—these outlanders look on us covetously, and too many Montanans stand ready to satisfy their hunger. Subdivisions sprout up border to border.

But the newcomer who today looks out from his place to the farthest limits of eyesight, tomorrow may find a neighbor's house in the forefront of his vision. Clutter comes, and traffic, and the unwelcome din of motorbikes, snowmobiles and outboard motors. The wildlife of yesterday disappears. So the dream ends but leaves a residue—the abuse of land and the pollution of waters and the diminishment of grandeur.

Do I exaggerate? Look to western Montana if you doubt. Visit elsewhere. Come to my old mountain cabin and see. On land adjacent to it, speculators have sold 25 lots. If they can qualify under the new state law, they will put up for sale 37 more. These are small plots, on limited acreage. Buyers sign covenants, agreeing to this stipulation and that, but who is to enforce the covenants? Not the speculators. When they sell out they'll get out, if they follow custom. These plots are on rock and jackpine land, worthless except for the privacy that buyers *won't* get, and except for seasonal grazing. Deer browse there, though, and occasionally bears venture forth from the mountains. But they won't if men come in numbers. Neither will the drainage of the Teton River improve, nor the quality of its water.

I do not mean to sound parochial or self-centered. What is happening close to me is happening elsewhere—almost, one might say, wherever a view exists and water can be found and a tree stands.

Dams come next in this reckoning, dams on streams great and small. I have to wonder about dams, knowing that engineers in their single-minded zeal have misfigured costs and benefits time after time. Their record shows their ratios to have been sadly wrong.

Right now there is agitation for a great dam on the Sun River in the neighborhood of Simms. It is referred to as the Lowry Dam. It would flood thousands of productive acres. By costly pumping, about that many other acres could be put under irrigation but only at a price so dear, according to my reports, that a couple of irrigation districts would go broke.

Proponents cite increased recreation as one of the prime benefits. Motorboating, I suppose, and water-skiing and swimming and fishing. Yes. Sunday carnivals all summer long. But the stream as it is provides fishing, and deer browse in its thickets and smaller wildlife lives on and near its course.

Cabin sites, too, I suppose, cabin sites for the urban weary. Yet any owner of a cabin at the edge of an artifical lake knows how uninviting and ugly the shores become as waters recede. He knows how dust blows once the reservoir level goes down. Towns downwind from dams know the dust problem, too. Ask residents to leeward of Canyon Ferry.

A big push for the Lowry Dam comes from property owners in West Great Falls, who built and bought where common sense ruled otherwise. Even after the great flood of 1964, construction proceeded, often on the very land that had been deep under water. Ignore the point that these people want the public to save them from their folly. At the cost of a dam, all West Great Falls could be relocated and rebuilt and owners paid a nice bonus besides.

Built, the dam won't discourage the strong winds from the west. Those winds will pick up dust from the dried shores and sweep it on. What, then, of the towns intervening? What of Sun River, Fort Shaw and Vaughn? What of West Great Falls and Great Falls itself? Must they, or some of them, live in a smother of dust? We can impound the waters, but we can't stay the wind.

I have good reason not to believe very much in flood control. In 1951, I traveled the Missouri River from Three Forks to Kansas City—by rowboat, outboard motor, steamboat and plane. I was a guest of the Army Corps of Engineers, later joined by the Bureau of Reclamation, and I saw the great dams and listened to their praises. At Kansas City, I saw the reclaimed land, bright with new factories and other installations. I saw that the Kansas River had been concreted in its channel. I saw miles and miles of restraining piles on the Missouri.

And the highest brass, seconded by other high brass, said to me, "That's what we ought to do everywhere—harness the rivers. Kansas City never again will have a major flood."

The very next year, Kansas City had the greatest flood in its history.

I do not trust the engineers, the great companies, the dealers in oil or power or timber. I don't trust them any more than I trust the makers of automobiles.

They have no morality. They have no commitment to earth, which to me is the prime morality. They drill and mine and cut and generate and lubricate the processes with empty promises. No, I don't trust them. And I don't much trust government, as it is, to govern itself.

Who trust, then? I think we come to the individual, to you and me. It is time we said: "No more of that!" It is time we elected men from among us who say what they mean and mean what they say. It is time we said: "An end to this damn equivocation! An end to weaseling! An end to compromise! You represent us or, by all that's holy, we'll recall you. We'll impeach you," making a quick procedure in that direction possible if it's not possible now.

In America we have had our millenium and were ignorant of it. We were all guilty of assaults on the land. We saw no end to earth's bounty. We don't see it yet. Not really. We go ahead. We grow. We bring to the markets, all markets, what we all want, prepared and packaged and tricked-out to our tastes.

Plenty more where that came from, we say. And if there's not plenty, we'll find a substitute.

But both the originals and their substitutes make harsh demands on the planet. Unchecked, the planet someday will run out of patience— which is to say, it will run out of what we have taken for granted. And then it will run out of us.

A man finds few absolutes in this life, look as he will. But one that forces itself on us is this: Progress leaves no retreat.

What has been done cannot be undone. Its ill effects may be ameliorated somewhat, but they can't be removed.

Whatever we do, whatever we plan to do, we should have that truth first in mind. Against it, people do say and will say, "We have to think first of man and his welfare." That happens to be precisely what I'm thinking about—man and his welfare. If we do not take care of Mother Earth, if we do not cherish and love and preserve her, then there is not only no welfare, but no future for man.

A. B. Guthrie, Jr. wrote this essay as the script for a talk delivered on August 27, 1977, in Bozeman, Montana, to a national gathering of the venerable angler's conservation group, Trout Unlimited.

TROUT. . .

UNLIMITED?

An old trapper I knew decided years ago that he had grown too old for that life. Winter after winter he had set his traps in the upper Teton River country and the drainage of the North Fork of the Sun River. Along the line he had slept in brush shelters, half dugouts and tents, no matter the weather.

So at last he came to town and rented a cabin. A couple of friends called on him soon afterwards. They found he had pitched a tent inside the cabin and asked him how come.

He answered, "Well, you see, when it rains, the roof she leaks a little."

I'll return to that subject later on.

There is no better an introduction to this talk than the first paragraph of Norman Maclean's fine book, *A River Runs Through It and Other Stories*, (The University of Chicago Press, 1976). That paragraph reads:

In our family, there was no clear line between religion and fly fishing. We lived at the junction of great trout rivers in western

Montana, and our father was a Presbyterian minister and a fly fisherman who tied his own flies and taught others. He told us about Christ's disciples being fishermen, and we were left to assume, as my brother and I did, that all first-class fishermen on the Sea of Galilee were fly fishermen and that John, the favorite, was a dry-fly fisherman.

My father was not a minister. He was a school principal who for 25 years taught the Bible class in the Methodist church.

His religious beliefs strained Methodist doctrine to the breaking point, for he was closer to being a Unitarian, but the standard of expected behavior was in nice accord. Until we kids at last succeeded in educating him, there were no playing cards in our house. We were not allowed to go to movies on Sunday, and when we went to Saturday-night dances we had to knock off—and I mean knock off—at the stroke of midnight.

But somehow fishing enjoyed an exemption from the list of Sunday forbidden things. We used to go three or four miles up the Teton River from Choteau, being sure of a good catch. We traveled by horse and buggy in those early days, later by Model-T Ford. On great occasions we went into the canyon of the Teton River or the canyons of Deep Creek a few miles south.

I have a picture of my father fishing in the North Fork of Deep Creek. There he is with his hat on, clothed in old trousers and old shoes. We couldn't afford waders and would have scorned them if we could. His shirt is white. And he wears a necktie—a necktie—not so much perhaps because the day is Sunday as because he would have felt undressed without one.

He scorned bait of any kind. If trout wouldn't come to a fly, let them stay in the water. But he always caught fish.

We always used wet flies, never having heard of dry ones, not until much later at least. But Dad could make a wet fly do as he wished. He could make it skitter, or flow or submerge, but he preferred to keep it on top and fluttering. His touch was gentle and expert. That ability always confounded me. He was no good with machinery, he couldn't tell which way to turn a nut, he never was sure of left and right, but how he could fish!

We seldom used a hook smaller than a #8. Sometimes we used #6s. Big hooks, you will say, but they worked.

A year ago a friend of mine in Glens Falls, New York, wanted to tie some flies for me. He asked what size I would like. When I said #8, he replied, "What are you fishing for, sharks?"

Though it has been quite a while since I wet a line, I found that in company with other fishermen who used much smaller hooks, I did as well or better than they.

But you must remember that, in those early days, all our trout were native cutthroats. If they are not the most sporty to catch, they remain the most tasty, better than German browns or brookies or rainbows.

What catches we used to make! Thirty or 40 per outing, for we never threw anything back except very small ones which Dad called peedads. What did we do with all those trout? I'll tell you: We ate them. We ate them all and enjoyed every bite. I think we would have consumed them all even had our circumstances been better. To this day I look askance at the man who loves to catch and keep trout and then has to canvass his neighbors to get rid of them, since he won't eat them himself.

I am led to believe that our earlier anglers were poets. Consider the names of the flies they swore by—most of which you won't find in today's lexicon of trout fishing. Listen to them: Royal Coachman, Grizzly King, Ginger Quill, the King and Queen of Waters, the lovely Parmachenee Belle. In the stead today you will find Woolly Worms, Muddler Minnows and, for all I know, Slimy Leeches. God help us. In a recent book, a good book called *The Challenge of the Trout*, I find only one of the names I've mentioned: the Royal Coachman.

What a lure! What a lure! It was my favorite. It was my old reliable. Dad, being a schoolman, preferred a Professor. My brother didn't care what just so he caught an occasional trout. But give me that old Royal Coachman, #8 hook, please, in any season, whatever the stage of the water, in any stream that I know.

The U.S. Fish and Game Commission will have to tell you when brookies were introduced into Montana. My memory tells me that in our section we began to catch them at about the time of World War I. They prospered. I think they are not quite so good a table fish as natives, and I know they are less wary, but they were welcome, and if the Commission is not planting them now, as I hear, I don't know why.

Not until about 1922 or 1923 did I get acquainted with the rainbow, itself a transplant, and now the most common trout in our waters, though the German brown, which I believe came along still later, may be coming close. I know nothing about the brown, never having caught one.

To catch the rainbow in flowing water we had to revise our technique just a little. We had to cast a longer line.

Some time before or about 1920 a large reservoir, called the Pishkun, was created in connection with the Sun River Irrigation Project, and rainbow trout were planted in it. There, as in all newly established lakes, the young trout thrived on fresh-water shrimp, and soon came bonanzas. Anglers of the region discovered what must have been the best trout fishing in the world—no fish under four pounds, ranging up to eight. A man was lucky to land three out of five strikes on light tackle. Every fisherman had a grasshopper net and a grasshopper box, which he kept filled. In waders, with a handful of hoppers, he baited the waters— he "chummed" them, to use eastern parlance—and, getting action, cast his hopper-laden hook to the rises.

There was no limit on catches, with the result of profligacy if not waste. Housewives canned the overcatch.

Those days—which lasted perhaps into the 1940s, if not so richly— are at an end. Somehow, whether by individuals or agencies, pike were planted in the Pishkun, and that's all you catch now. Beaching a pike is about as exciting as snaring a sucker.

Years after the great days I built a house on the banks of the upper Teton, where I live now, and every day I look and mourn, for the stream is dead.

It began dying even as we made our fine catches. It was being overgrazed and then over-tilled, and increasing diversion for irrigation left the channel dry near town, in the very stretches I used to hike to, often alone, happy in the knowledge I would catch fish. A fish-and-game crew came along and shocked a mile of the stream, where it still ran, and by report came up with one little brookie, and it several years old. No feed, said the crew. No use to stock that river. No feed. Nothing for trout where trout used to flourish. We still caught a few, though, a few for a while.

Then, in the early '50s, along came a flood, not the biggest on record or the biggest still to be, but big enough to arouse concern. The Army Corps of Engineers entered the act then, those all-knowing men who in their wisdom do things wrong. With bulldozers and draglines and whatnot, they gouged out a straight chute for the stream, a chute several miles long just upstream from Choteau. "Flood control," they said. "Protect the town," they said. "Protect the property owner."

A little later, as the years go, the Forest Service, that once-high-minded protector of our natural resources, authorized clear-cutting on the headwaters of the Teton in country so fragile that a lifetime isn't long enough for a man to see a tree grow to maturity. Two lifetimes, perhaps. Perhaps more.

So everything was fine. Town protected from flood. Mills supplied with poor-grade timber.

Everything was fine until 1964, when the greatest flood on record swept down the Teton, tearing away all undergrowth as it went, and visited the town. The once-lovely stream has no trout pools in it now and no shade for trout. It flows through a wide bed of gravel where nothing grows except, just this year, for the yellow clover that the Soil Conservation Service was wise enough to sow.

Such a flood, the wise men said, was to be expected no more than once in 500 years. They didn't say in just *what* year in each span of time. They didn't say that *two* such floods could occur, one right after the other, and still average out over the centuries as an exceedingly rare event.

It's lucky for them that they allowed leeway, for just 11 years later, in 1975, came a flood much like its immediate predecessor.

Choteau has been declared flood-prone, and the citizens are greatly concerned with the classification. Not so, they contend in the face of the facts. Some more earth-moving, some more flood control, has been authorized just west of town. But I am aware of no effort to get at the manmade, if subsidiary, causes of floods.

Against the forces of destruction we are few and feeble. How can we alone discourage developers? How can we deter or guide the rich and omnipotent highway department? How can we alter the course of the U.S. Forest Service, whose policies are made in Washington?

While Trout Unlimited, while you members or some of you, seek to repair the ruination wrought in the East, we Westerners fight a lonely battle so that you, and we, can enjoy what you once enjoyed but can enjoy no more—except in our waters.

Looking at what has been done in Montana, looking at what we hope to do, I fear sometime we are only pitching tents because the roof, she leaks a little. We must *repair* that roof, but how? Only through the wide awareness that such organizations as yours can encourage. Only by persuasion, only by standing up and being counted, only by example and publicity, by litigation if necessary, only by bringing force to bear against opposing forces, only by monies from such organizations as yours.

I want no more trout waters to go the way of the Teton. I look at the stream, hard by my house, and I can see us fishing again, my brother, my father and I, and I can see Dad bringing a trout to shore, his tie dark against the white of his shirt, and we eat lunch on the river bank, and the sun shines soft on lively waters, and, looking, I think of the food chain and know that the health of fish is the health of man.

Inflated prices for land and machinery, usurious interst rates and high operating costs: In the following essay—read at a symposium on the family farm held in Lewistown, Montana, on March 27, 1980—A. B. Guthrie, Jr. already had identified and was calling public attention to the very problems that, by the mid-1980s, would lead to the bankruptcy of thousands of traditional American farming families.

PROGRESS
AND THE
FAMILY FARM

You may call me old-fashioned. I believe in the family farm and the farm family. I believe that values are established there as nowhere else—values such as the felt need for cooperation, the knowledge of nature, of land, of plants and animals, respect for the work ethic, which a great many people are scoffing at today, and the knowledge of the importance of family ties. Where but on a farm or ranch would youngsters acquire such ready understanding of life and death, of matings and births?

Believing in the farm family, I also believe in small towns. I prefer them to cities.

If I am old-fashioned, it is because I was born that way, not because I am old—though the Lord knows I am. But I don't feel so old as another speaker implied a few years ago. He called me a "living legend." I tell you, that shook me up. It was as if I ought to be stuffed and displayed with extinct birds, like the ivory-billed woodpecker. Just last week, while I was signing books, a buyer asked if I wouldn't put down my age along with the inscription. I acknowledge my age and so put it down, but the request was impudent. If I'd had time for second thoughts, I would have written: "I was a close friend of General Custer."

As a boy and young man I did a lot of rough work, on farms and ranches in Montana and Mexico and at a feed mill in New York State. Then, when I landed a job as a reporter in Kentucky, I noted with amazement how soft and weak were the hands of the other reporters and how little they knew of the physical techniques of living. I counted myself lucky that I had done that earlier work. That's one of the values of farm life—to know hard work and to know how to do it.

These days I fear for the family farm. Land prices are incredibly high, high beyond any hope of profit from investment. Machinery costs a great deal of money. How much does it take for a young man, starting from scratch, to establish himself? Will a quarter-million do it? Doubtful. And where does a young fellow get that kind of money? Borrowing won't help him, even if he can arrange to borrow, not with interest rates amounting to usury. Perhaps he can hope to inherit, but inheritances diminish according to the number of heirs, with the result that farms and ranches are often sold on the death of owners—sold to syndicates or wealthy men seeking tax losses or to the Hutterites who always seem to have plenty of money.

I am saying that land prices are crazy and interest rates insufferable. It used to be said in a more moderate time that a rancher did reasonably well if he earned 3% of his investment. At the present scale of things, if land prices, machinery costs and operation are included, he's lucky to keep his shirt.

The increases in costs parallel, ironically, an increase in the number of young people who want to be farmers. I know some of them. I wish they had a chance. Their interest in living on and from the land is a healthy thing. It would be good for the future, for the nation, if these people could find locations.

If I had answers to the situation I've described, I would make a great Secretary of Agriculture—but I wouldn't be appointed. Big government seems not to approve of competence. But to recognize a bad situation is a step toward solving it, and I trust that someone will come up with answers.

I want to digress here and talk about progress, speaking out of a personal conviction that progress leaves us no retreat. Or perhaps I am proceeding, for the family farmer's problems today are the outgrowth of the process we call progress. All change means some destruction, most progress is goodbye.

The prime fact is that we are deluding ourselves. We subscribe to that hoary myth that bigger means better. Usually it means worse. Chambers of commerce in Montana, as elsewhere, talk about bringing in industry and broadening the tax base, by which they imply lower taxes. A man has only to look at the record to spot this deception. New York City has a lot of industry. So does Cleveland. And the tax rates in those places would stagger Montanans. Yet in spite of those rates, both cities are on the edge of financial ruin.

Centered industry, masses of people, mean social unrest. They mean high crime rates. They mean slums. They mean periodic unemployment. They mean strikes. They mean more welfare and more taxes. They mean pollution of land, water and sky.

For an example of pollution in Montana one might cite fast-growing Missoula. Otherwise, it is a pleasant and well-ordered town, but the air is so thick that a man needs four lungs to survive and even then he may not.

Another aspect of progress disheartens me. That is the loss of good, productive land to multi-lane highways, to suburbs, to the work of developers with an eye on the buck who sell plots for cabins and summer homes on acreage where cattle recently grazed and wild game ranged. How much good land is lost annually I don't know. But it is substantial.

We look back and take pride in the settlement of America. Rightly so. Less than two centuries after the Revolution, we had settled the land. Hard on the heels of Lewis and Clark came other explorers, came fur hunters, came the Oregon and California pushes of men, came mills and plows and industries and cities. It was a glorious time, if not pleasant for everybody. In the long roll of history never had a continent so quickly been put to use. The record shines. We crossed mountains, plains, rivers, lakes, forests, no matter how formidable, and wherever conditions were suitable, we planted the seeds and tended the shoots of civilization. It was a dream realized. It is a dream to be dreamed again, if in a different direction.

The dream had its nightmares, though.

One of the greatest of explorers was also a student of land, water, climate, plants and animals. He reported officially what he saw and believed—and was largely ignored. It is a shame. He was a great American, and his name, John Wesley Powell, is largely lost, though I am sure some of you have heard of him and speakers here before me may have talked of him.

After a careful survey of the Great Plains, Powell recommended, in the late 1870s, that the standard family unit in the West should be no less than 2,560 acres. A mere quarter-section was no good.

But Congress was dominated then, and still is, by easterners and midwesterners. They didn't go along with Powell. One-hundred and sixty acres was a pretty fair chunk of land in lush and fertile country watered by frequent rains. So 160 acres became the homesteader's share of free land. Later, that figure was doubled but was still far too little.

It should be remarked that Powell thought mostly of livestock raising, not cereal production. Incidentally, I suppose we might quarrel with him a bit. Twenty-five-hundred and sixty acres seems to me rather small for a going cattle or sheep ranch. But let's not quibble. Powell had vision. He lived long before the development of summer fallowing but, even so, he warned against alkalinization on irrigated fields. We know it all too well these days as saline seep.

The homesteaders came, as everybody knows, and most of them withered in the sun and wind and were blown away. The tougher ones, which may mean those better situated, increased their holdings by one means or another. One trick was for homesteaders to persuade townsmen or drifting cowpunchers to file on land adjacent to theirs, then turn it over to them eventually at a dollar or less an acre. A good many Montana ranches developed in this way. I know of a few in my home country. There was a bit of chicanery here, and evasion of the intent of the law, but what could you expect when Congress was stupid enough to rule that 160 acres meant a Montana farm?

To some extent, however, those early Congresses are to be excused. They saluted the sturdy yeoman, even if they did nothing much else for him.

Yes, I have been around for a long time. But I was a boy once, before most of you were born. My home was in Choteau, Montana, and my place in the universe lovely with the natural bounty around me. We were almost poor, but I was rich. I looked at the great sky and breathed the tonic air, and the world was good. I drank, belly down, from rivers and creeks and ditches, with never a consequence except the remembered taste of good water. I wandered in the open fields. I walked half a mile and caught a creelful of trout. I rustled through the cinquefoil and flushed a covey of prairie chickens and shot a couple and took them home, proud. I found ducks in the potholes, ducks in the beaver ponds, ducks along the little streams, and I brought them down, too, and added them to our larder, feeling self-sufficient in my unchanging world.

With other boys I swam in streams where the current had scoured swimming holes, swam in water so clear that, opening my eyes while submerged, I could see the patterns on minnows, in water so cold that we built bonfires on shore to warm ourselves by.

My family had a horse, old Fox, and a buggy, and we got places with them, satisfied with our pace, glad after a long haul to smell the good smell of pine, glad to see, glinting blue in the Teton, a hole we surely would fish. My eyes could see far, unobstructed by the structures of men, and so I had room for dreams.

I cannot do those things again, nor are they there to do. The streams I knew then, today run polluted and slow, or wild in the spring and dry the next month, and the promising trout holes still to be found are empty of fish. The potholes mostly are dry, the works of man block my eye, and a few minutes in an automobile take me joylessly where I went joyful behind old Fox, though the trip required half a day.

Yet not everything is lost. The air around my old home is still clean and tonic. Ear Mountain stands to the west, guarantee of eternity, and I imagine that industrious boys can still find fish to catch in the summer and, in the fall, see a cottontail sitting. Boys can still dream their boys' dreams.

Musing this way, I wish all of our towns had libraries and good ones. I wish our standards of primary education were higher. They are low by any ratings except possibly the teachers'. I would welcome the town or county brass bands as of yore. For youngsters, I would try to provide more clean recreation. These days, only the bars are alive after dark, and the ambition of kids is to grow old enough to buy a drink. I wish for a return of the local flour mill and the creamery, and to hell with Pillsbury and Kraft. I would festoon the main streets with trees.

I would preserve what remains of the old riches. I would save those encouragements, those fulfillments, those opportunities for the boys who will be me again. Posterity owes us nothing. The truth is quite different: We owe a good world to posterity.

I can and do hope for a return of the old, bold American spirit, directed now not to the exploitation of the country but to the good care of it. In some part, our mistakes can be redressed. We can make the streams flow clean again. We can reestablish the damaged watersheds and so minimize the danger of spring floods while ensuring year-around flow. Given back our old confidence, we may find the answer to saline seep. We may find how to put aspiring young people on the land they hunger for. I pray for that return of confidence and its accomplishments.

That would be progress.

Guthrie composed this compact essay as a statement to be read at the Montana Governor's Award Ceremonies, held in January 1982.

WHY
DO I LOVE
THE LAND?

Why do I love the land? Why do I embrace the idea of wilderness?

There is no one answer. The answer lies in details.

It is cold in Montana today, cold on the high plateau where we live almost within the shadow of Ear Mountain. As my father did before me, I look often to the mountain, perhaps hoping to borrow a bit of Everlasting from it.

Snow lies deep on meadow and hill, the Teton River is frozen hard, bank to spreading bank, and the air is quiet with arctic chill. The jackpines stand dark against the white. They are survivors, impervious to the whims of weather. The largest of them number their ages in scores, even hundreds, of years. A scientist once wanted to take a core sample from one of them and thus establish its age. He said the tree wouldn't suffer. I wouldn't let him drill. It is too easy for men to kill things, too often in the name of progress.

A stranger might look on the land, on the great reaches of snow, and think all is desolation, all waste, never to come alive. But under the smother of snow, defiant of the fingers of chill, seeds and roots and rodents await the touch of spring.

Before long now, the wild goose will come honking from the south, and pasqueflowers will push their lavender blooms through the warming soil. Then will come moss campion and wild forget-me-nots and dwarf phlox, and the land will be a glory of red-purple, blue and white. These early arrivals grow low, and I call them carpet flowers. They cannot live under the cut of the plow, the tramp of feet or too many munching mouths. Walk carefully. Do not disturb. Just look and wonder.

Nor is the flowering season done then. Bluebonnets will deck roadways and ridges, and balsam root splash yellow on the hills. And Columbian ground squirrels will be frolicking on the knolls.

With the flowers will come the birds—warblers, white-crowned sparrows, robins, redstarts and a host of others, small and big.

I sit and I walk and I look and I listen, and do not ask why I love the land. I only know that I love it.

John Burroughs, the naturalist, once wrote, "The longer I live, the more my mind dwells on the beauty and the wonder of the world."

I embrace that statement, here in Montana, here in the dead of winter.

Bozeman, April 29, 1983: Shortly before delivering this talk as the capstone speaker for a lecture series cosponsored by the Bridger Environmental Education Program and the Montana Committee for the Humanities, Guthrie had undergone surgery for a skin cancer, leaving one arm temporarily in a sling. In spite of his 82 years, the physical drain of recent surgery and 17 days of hospitalization, plus the discomfort and inconvenience of the sling, Guthrie stood for 40 minutes to deliver this talk—which he and Carol Guthrie promptly dubbed his "one-armed speech." Excerpts from the talk were printed in Bozeman and Billings newspapers, and the entire text went on the wireservice.

HERE AND

HEREAFTER

Both the Puritans, who landed on our shores in 1607, and the Pilgrims, who arrived in 1620, looked on the New World as an exclusive gift from God, as a sort of second chance at the Garden of Eden.

In a sense, though they couldn't know what lay westward, they were right, for never in the history of mankind had a land so varied, so rich, so promising, lain before seekers of better and more profitable lives.

In the December 1982 number of *Defenders*, the magazine of Defenders of Wildlife, an article entitled "Trouble in the Tongass," authored by Joe Cone and Roger Di Silvestro, began:

> When the first colonists arrived in North America they en-
> countered something for which neither their memories nor their
> imaginations had prepared them. . . . It was forest, virgin forest
> virtually untouched by the ambitions of mankind. Within the
> region which would one day comprise the 48 contiguous states,

almost 500 million acres of deep forests stretched from the Atlantic to the Mississippi.

The push inland took a short breather then, for the colonists had to accustom themselves to a new land and a new way of living. More, they were few and had to wait on natural increase and immigration before venturing farther, though a few bold ones were already poking at the barriers of the Alleghenies and the Appalachians.

But the westward movement, if slowed for a while, was inevitable. Ways were found through and around the mountains. Pittsburgh, at first a fort at the headwaters of the Ohio River, came into being in 1755. Daniel Boone, in 1775, blazed the Wilderness Road into Tennessee and Kentucky. Louisville was laid out in 1786, Cincinnati in 1788.

It was a great experience, floating down the Ohio by flatboat or broadhorn. On every bank rose the majesty of the forest, crowned by the queen of them all, the tulip poplar. Just one of these giants, the settlers discovered, would provide enough timber for a house and a barn with something left over. And it was pleasant wood to work with. There were sycamores, maples, walnuts, locusts—hardwoods and softwoods beyond calculation. Until they learned better, the home-seekers thought land that grew trees wouldn't grow crops or garden stuff. Then they cut clearings.

Land of disputed ownership lay farther west. The Spanish, the French and the British at one time or another laid claim to all or parts of it. Then came the Louisiana Purchase and the expedition of Lewis and Clark, begun in 1804. The fur hunters, the beaver trappers, followed hard on their heels. They went up the Missouri, the Yellowstone and their tributaries and south to the Wind River Range and the Popo Agie and, always venturesome, discovered or rediscovered South Pass and the western waters, finding Great Salt Lake, the Columbia drainage, California itself.

They found the routes and blazed the trails, to their chagrin, giving impetus to the movements of humbler men, to seekers of homes and farms and an ordered way of life far different from their own. Hardly had the mountain men given up to age and change than the great migration to Oregon and, if a man chose, to California, began. That was in the 1840s, and by the end of that decade the Oregon Trail was not a single road but a big, wide number of roads all bound for the same places. Detours and forced digressions from the original accounted for the variety.

Those early migrants had difficulties. They had come from forested regions and here, beyond the hundredth meridian, was almost treeless land, relieved rarely by fringes of cottonwood and willows along the channels of streams. It was the Great American Desert, so-called, and so in fact in the travelers' minds. They used buffalo chips for fires and made toward the mountains with what haste they could manage. Twelve miles by prairie schooner wasn't too bad a day. Along the way, if not always, were buffalo, tens of thousands of them, to be shot and cooked for eager stomachs.

Later on, the descendants of these men and women, together with thousands more pouring in from the east, would discover that most of the Great American Desert wasn't desert at all. It would grow cereals, provide grazing for livestock, nourish gardens.

Gold was discovered in California, in Montana, in Colorado and elsewhere, and here came the prospectors, the get-rich-quick hopefuls, an addition to population, a great tributary to the stream of western movement.

Human populations, wherever found, need food, need good red meat, and it didn't take the Texas trail drivers long to learn that there was profit in bypassing the railhead towns in Kansas, driving on to summer pasture in the short-grass country and then trailing back to the railroad.

From that experience grew what has been called the days of the cattlemen. Vast herds of beef were brought to the plains of Wyoming and Montana and parts of Colorado and the Dakotas, there to remain year-round, save for those sent to market. It had been proven to everyone's satisfaction that cattle could survive the northern winters. Natural increase would more than offset any winterkill and calf mortality. Syndicates, organized in England and Scotland, invested. So did wealthy Texans. The foreigners were a sophisticated and often titled lot. The Cheyenne Club was as cosmopolitan as Delmonicos. The grass was free. Hail, fortune!

I am skipping over the Revolution, the Civil War, the coming of the railroads, the subjugation of the Indians and the advent of the homesteaders. They were important, God knows, but are not necessary to my theme.

All the years of the frontier were exuberant times, times of beckoning fortune. If not right in one place, opportunity and wealth lay just over the hill, in the next region, in the next state or territory, from horizon to horizon, from sea to shining sea. The world had caught on. Along with some well-to-do who hoped to do better yet, there arrived on our shores the oppressed, the destitute, the weary, all with hope in their eyes. They came from England, Scotland and Ireland, from Germany, Scandinavia, Russia and Poland, from virtually every country in Europe. From the other direction came Japanese and Chinese.

By the 1890s, the American frontier was gone. Never in world history had so vast a region been settled so quickly.

Hopeful, ebullient times. Ambitious and venturesome men. A land rich beyond thought. Oh, boy!

But the new Garden of Eden had too many apples and too many Eves. In their train, the fortune-seekers left damage and loss beyond assessment. They left destruction and pollution and denuded land. They left cesspools of poison. They left toxic waste dumps now estimated to number more than 14,000. They had no time or inclination to think of results.

Defenders goes on to say: "By the early years of the 20th century virtually all of the forest in the northeastern and central states would be cut. Within the next 50 years it would vanish almost everywhere."

Save for a few remnants, the buffalo, those thousands and thousands of them, were all gone. They were killed in great numbers by so-called sportsmen, but the real work of extinction was done by hide-hunters who stripped robes from the carcasses and left the good meat to the wolves and coyotes. From a good stand a hunter might kill 40 of the beasts and never move except for reloading. The government looked kindly on this enterprise; starving Indians would be easier to corral on reservations. A good Indian was a begging Indian.

I find no evidence that observers, coming along after much of the forest had been cut and the grass grazed to the roots, noticed any diminution in stream flow or the increasing occurrence of flood. If they did, they probably blamed nature.

But the first journals give river and stream widths far greater than exist today. To be sure, most, though not all, of the measurements were estimates, yet all had a remarkable sameness. The water courses were clearer, too, and travelers drank from them without fear or misfortune. If someone got sick from the water, it was usually the result of drinking from alkali lakes, which caused diarrhea. Cholera broke out now and then, but it was the doings of man, not nature.

Love of the land was an emotion hardly in evidence. By tradition, if in rocky New England a farmer wore out one piece of land, he moved to another—an example too often followed by tillers of the Great Plains. Mine it and leave it. There was plenty more.

I have just returned from Iowa, whose soil was once as rich as any on God's green earth. Yet a good corn crop or a good soybean crop there today depends on fertilizer, a lot of it. The papers and television screens are full of advertisements for the stuff. And now, out of experience, Hawkeyes are becoming concerned about soil loss through wind and erosion.

The mountain man trapped out the beaver. The hide-hunter exterminated the buffalo. The gold miner took out the gold and departed for other occupations or climes. There may be one or two small operations still in the Mother Lode country of California, but it or they are all. No gold to speak of left in Colorado or Montana. And the silver from the great Comstock Lode in Virginia City has long since been mined and minted. To come to more recent times, the copper-bearing richest hill on earth, in Butte, has been looted and left, an incredible eyesore.

The day of the cattlemen: It came to an end in the bitter winter of 1886–87. The cattle, already poor in flesh because of overgrazing, died by the thousands. Foreign investors went belly-up. A new time had arrived, the time of fences and hay for winter feed.

I look around me today and I see continued abuse of land. In two instances not far from my home, thousands of acres of good grazing land have been plowed to grow cereals already overabundant. The winds blow hard there. They will whip the topsoil away. In time I expect those acres to grow into weeds. It takes a long, long time for nature to restore herself.

The trapper, the explorer, the settler, the cowboy, the entrepreneur, each had a strong sense of what were his rights. By George, if he owned a piece of land, it was his to do with as he pleased! If he grazed it to the roots, who could say him nay? His home was his castle, his land his domain. If neighbors objected to certain practices, that was their headache. What if a man built a smelter? It was on his own property. These rights were as fixed as the right of the cowboy to drink himself drunk.

By extension, these rights applied to the corporation. It owned land or machinery or mineral rights or processing plants and, owning them, could do as it pleased. Call this feeling of rights the pioneer or cowboy ethic. For years, appealing to what it called the "cow country," the Anaconda Copper Company was able to dominate the state of Montana. It has pulled out now, having taken all the good from the richest hill on earth. Chet Huntley called Anaconda the greatest friend Montana ever had. I can do without friendships like that.

So today we are gathered hoping to preserve something of what remains pristine in America, something to delight eyes and comfort souls, something natural in which natural life can live.

More than that, we want clean water and clean air. We want to put an end to acid rain, to preserve the national parks, to remove or make safe the toxic dumps of industry. It is a big order. How can we act effectively against fat purses and greedy ambitions? Arrayed against us are the oil companies, the mining interests, the timber cutters, the administration.

Our hope is the increasing numbers of us, the strength of our wills.

That will of ours has been made manifest recently: We shot down the mismanagers of the Environmental Protection Agency. Anne Gorsuch Burford is gone and her cohorts with her. Against the stubborn resistance of the Reagan Administration, which still insists that these people did no wrong, we prevailed. And when it is suggested that clean air and clean water regulations be weakened, the American people rise up and say, "No. By God, we want a healthy environment. Lay off!"

But admittedly, the way is hard. The president opposes us, as is to be expected from a man who said that if you've seen one redwood, you've seen them all. John Muir would not have agreed.

With the EPA taken care of, we hope, I suggest we take aim next at the Interior Department headed by the ineffable James Gains Watt. He says he's an environmentalist. Yep, and the Soviets say they are democratic. Watt's executive department is filled with people whose experience and associations hardly suggest a devotion to clean air and water or the preservation of what remains pristine in America. Take a look. In charge of the national forests: John B. Crowell, former general counsel to the Louisiana Pacific Corporation. Solicitor in the Department of the Interior: William H. Coldiron, vice-chairman of the board of Montana Power Company. Director of the Bureau of Land Management: Robert F. Burford, former spokesman for the Sagebrush Rebellion.

The list goes on and on. Watt is only one of 16 top officials nominated by President Reagan and confirmed by the Senate. Of the 16, 11 of the original appointees had prior professional relationships with industries that either lease federal land or have a direct interest in departmental decisions.

There, then, is the target, headed by Mr. Watt, a born-again man who believes that the earth may die in his lifetime. So he sings with Omar, "Ah, make the most of what ye yet may spend." I have the happy feeling that Watt will be terminated, one way or the other, before the planet melts. Take aim, you people.

Here we are, beleaguered but not dismayed, twice armed because we are right. If propaganda has tried to make "conservationist" a dirty word, I am proud to march under the dirty banner. Though I am sometimes accused of being soft-headed or an obstacle to progress, I still call for a curse on the despoilers. I am not lenient enough to say, "Forgive them, Father, for they know not what they do." For all his compassion, Jesus still drove the money-changers from the temple.

With this essay, Guthrie commented on the fate of the grizzly bear. The magazine's editors subtitled the piece: "One of America's great authors reflects on a giant of the wild." It appeared originally in the July 24, 1983, issue of Parade Magazine.

REQUIEM FOR OLD EPHRAIM

It is night in the high country, and three of us are sitting around a campfire, ready to cook buffalo meat. On the edge of light, indistinct at first, rears a grizzly bear, standing higher than a horse, and I am awed and half-scared and wholly admiring. We don't raise our rifles. There he is, the tips of his coat lightened by the flare of the fire, a creature of dream and myth, made real now and instinct with the life of the wild. He lets himself down on all fours and vanishes into the dark, and the hand that I have on my gun lifts and gestures in thanks for the gift of his appearance.

The scene is imaginary, born of nights in the open along the headwaters of Rocky Mountain streams, of long talks with old-timers, of a lifelong interest in the ways and fortunes of the fur hunters who lived long before me. But if the scene is fiction, it is fact in the experiences of older men, most of them now dead.

The grizzly is a living, snorting incarnation of the wildness and grandeur of America. He has been known, both in esteem and in dread, as the silvertip, the great white bear and, by the mountain men of the 1830s, as Old Ephraim.

Once grizzly numbers were many. Once his domain was not exclusively the mountains but the high plains and prairies. He was known even east of the Mississippi, where he fingered out along the streams. But west of the Missouri and over the mountains to the Pacific was his real empire. At the beginning of the 18th century, there were maybe 50,000 grizzlies west of the Mississippi. The men of the Lewis and Clark Expedition killed 13 at the Great Falls of the Missouri in present-day Montana. They killed for sport, not meat, and a kind of sport it was, for their single-shot muzzle-loaders were hardly sure killers, and the dangerous encounters left the riflemen with the sweetened memories of terror.

One hundred and eighty-some years have passed, and the grizzly has been driven to the last refuge of the mountains. How many remain? The numbers are subject to estimate. In his refuge in the American West, the total has dwindled to 600 or perhaps 1200, and these are not prospering. The figures are those of Dr. Charles Jonkel, staff member of the University of Montana and director of the Border Grizzly Project. He says that the figures are loose and may be off at either end of the scale. Of these survivors, 80 percent are to be found in Montana, the rest in Wyoming, Idaho and Washington. There are from 165 to 350 in Yellowstone National Park, and maybe 200 in Glacier National Park. Not a one is left in California, and his existence is doubtful at best in Colorado or the Southwest.

I live in grizzly bear country, along the Front Range of the Rocky Mountains in north-central Montana. Five miles from my home, straight line, lies the Pine Butte Swamp, now owned by the Nature Conservancy. Every spring, grizzlies come here, venturing out onto the high plains. In the swamp grows the green stuff that their hungry systems need.

Green stuff in the spring. But the grizzly is not particular about his diet. He will eat insects, berries, tubers and meat, fresh or stale, as well as greens.

Ten to 20 bears visit the swamp annually, some spending the summers there, one perhaps staying the year round. Of the 100 or so bears that Dr. Jonkel and his staff have trapped in Montana and equipped with radio devices so as to keep track of their wanderings, five have been located in the swamp.

On the way from the mountains to the swamp, the bears travel two courses—from the canyons of the Teton River and those of Willow Creek to destination. My home rests on or close to the Teton route. I know they come, I know they've been near, but I don't see them, for these are unspoiled mountain bears. They travel by dark or in the cover of draws, wanting no trouble. When I go out at night, careful only to make enough noise to announce my coming, I walk without fear. I won't startle a bear if he's there or be at all likely to come between mother and cub.

The animal's reputation for savagery has been heightened by tragedies in Yellowstone and Glacier parks. In the summer of 1980, three people were killed by grizzlies in Glacier, and a woman was killed there in 1976. At Yellowstone in 1972, a man was killed by a grizzly. And more recently there have been others. But in the majority of cases—not all—the human victims have acted in ignorance or rash heedlessness.

All the same, the grizzly is a fierce and awesome adversary. An adult male will weigh from 400 to 600 pounds, a female from 300 to 400. Standing at a stretch, a big bear will measure nine feet tall. That's not all. As a horse trainer would say, the grizzly has a lot of early foot. His bursts of speed are short but fast. He has been clocked at 40 miles an hour, more than enough to run down a deer. And he has big claws, a big mouth and teeth, and a hug to crush ribs.

Along the Front Range of the Rockies, in the 150 miles of country I know best, I recall just one man-bear encounter outside of those incidents that occurred in Yellowstone and Glacier. A sheepman awakened one night to the sounds of disturbance in his band. He seized his rifle, not recalling he had but one shell in it, and went out. The bear was there all right. He shot it. It went down, only to rise and charge as he approached. It mauled him and went away. Then it returned and mauled him some more as he tried to get back to camp. But Broadhurst Smith was tough stuff. He survived. When I saw him later, the only signs of the struggle were scars on his bald head where the scalp had been refitted to his skull.

Sheepmen and sheepherders, like Smith, threaten the grizzly. Full knowing about the likely presence of bears there, they insist on grazing their bands on the rich uplands, the sweet mountain meadows. Bears do kill and eat sheep, as well as bigger domestic animals sometimes, and the temptation of the herder is to shoot first and claim protection afterward.

They are not the only threats to the existence of the species. Man's encroachment on his habitat is more important. The habitat becomes more and more restricted, and clamorous with machinery. A female grizzly needs 30 square miles to move around in, a male more than that. The reproductive rate is low—six cubs in the natural lifetime of a healthy mother. Here, Dr. Jonkel hopes, nature may answer by raising the rate.

A further danger, perhaps just as great, is the poacher. He covets claws, later to be fashioned into jewelry. He covets the gallbladder. It is reported that, dried and ground, this organ commands fancy prices on the Far Eastern market as an aphrodisiac. Collectors want the hides.

Legal hunting, at least in Montana, is a minor concern. The state sets an annual bear-death limit of 25 from all causes, such as illness, natural death or accident. Hunters with legal permits kill perhaps 10 a year of that number. [Editor's note: As of April 1987, the limit for human-caused grizzly deaths before hunting is stopped is 14 total or six females, whichever comes first.]

Even so, grizzlies are being killed every day, openly and secretly. The bear has been designated as a threatened—but not endangered—species, and he does have more friends than enemies. Among these friends are the Audubon Society and various wilderness groups.

Montana legislators recently learned about public sentiment in regard to the bear. The question arose as to what should be the official Montana animal, the grizzly or the elk. It appeared that the State Legislature might designate the elk. But then hundreds of schoolchildren showed up last spring to demand that the bear be chosen. The legislators had no choice.

And it is just this sort of action that is the key to the grizzly's survival. With enough money and enough enforcing legislation, the grizzly might endure indefinitely in the open, but only the people can make it happen.

Despite all these efforts on behalf of Old Ephraim, men who are not so optimistic predict that he will be gone from the lower 48 states within the next 35 years. If they are right, there will have disappeared from our wilds the grandest animal Americans have known. And old men, their eyes lost in the past, will be saying, "I remember. . ."

Living, as he does, at the heart of Montana's Front Range grizzly habitat, A. B. Guthrie, Jr. has long been actively involved in the ongoing scuffle between friends of the bear and the "three-S" crowd (Shoot, Shovel and Shut-up). In the Choteau area this controversy has grown to be highly divisive, in some cases setting friend against friend, neighbor against neighbor. In early 1985, Guthrie submitted the following letter to U.S. Senator Max Baucus (D-Montana) to be entered as testimony in hearings on grizzly bear management scheduled to be held in July 1985 before the Subcommittee on Environmental Pollution of the Committee on Environment and Public Works, United States Senate (first session, Great Falls, Montana). The letter was subsequently published in the official records of that hearing (S. Hrg. 99–279).

THE

GRIZZLY BEAR

SYNDROME

In the past two years a sort of hysteria, promoted by extremists, has pervaded Teton County. It might be called the grizzly bear syndrome.

It is true that in those two years the grizzly has come from the mountains out on the plains as it has not done before in the memory of living observers. Yet in that time the damage has been limited to a few commercial beehives and 12 sheep. Except for the fright a bear near his doorstep naturally caused a farmer, the grizzly has not harmed one human being, though heaven knows humans have provoked it enough.

A recent example was an incident east of Fairfield where the bear just mentioned, chased by authorities who sought to tranquilize it, took refuge in a windbreak. The word got around, and people jammed in cars and hurried to the scene, and some of them let their children get out and throw rocks into the timber. The bear thus had reason to come out charging, for even a cow, pestered enough, will go on the peck. But this bear stayed in the windbreak and finally was tranquilized.

The case has a sequel. The bear, transplantd to the headwaters of the Flathead, came back to Teton County and in the neighborhood of the town of Bynum raided some beehives and killed six sheep. Tranquilized again, it was taken to Missoula and put in the charge of Dr. Charles Jonkel, widely known authority on grizzlies. He is engaged in a program to induce fear of humans in problem bears. By latest report, of the nine he has treated only two have been troublesome afterwards. That's not proof of final success, of course, but it gives reason for hope.

The story just told about the Fairfield bear and the crowd that gathered has been much the same elsewhere. Let it be known that a grizzly is in sight somewhere, and whole families leap into cars and go hence. They are not only curious but, I think, also drawn by the exciting prospect of a bit of danger.

All manner of rumors have circulated in Choteau. One man reported he had counted nine grizzlies at a feedlot about eight miles north of town. Another reported signs of a grizzly right in town. The reports were without foundation, except perhaps for the sighting of sign in town, but it is in the nature of people to want to believe.

One factor—in addition to dry seasons and the want of wild fruits and tubers in the mountains—one factor that attracts grizzlies to the plains is the careless manner in which ranchers and feedlots dispose of dead livestock. They leave the animals out in the field or dump them into open trenches. When an east wind blows, the scent carries west to the bears.

It is characteristic of the extremists to blame the bears entirely, not the dead-animal practices. It is also characteristic to look for scapegoats. In this instance one scapegoat is the Nature Conservancy and the Pine Butte Swamp that it owns. It is no use to point out that the swamp and its environs have been managed no differently as to bears than they were for years under private ownership. Hot heads can't tolerate cold facts.

Yet the rancher who loses stock on private land should be paid damages if he is reasonably careful in the disposal of dead livestock. Nothing should be paid to those who lease public lands in and near grizzly habitat. They went in with their eyes open and took their chances and suffered losses. They bet and lost. No one repays a losing Las Vegas gambler.

The hysteria remains, fed by extremists, rumor-mongers and sometimes by newspapers. The news story about the Fairfield bear was sober and well-balanced in *The Great Falls Tribune*, but the sensation-seeking headline writer had in black letters something like this: "Grizzly Wreaks Havoc in Fairfield Area." What nonsense!

It is equally foolish that people keep asking me: "What about bears around your place?" I live rather close to Pine Butte Swamp and closer yet to the canyons of the Teton River and not once have I seen a grizzly in the neighborhood.

The extremists give a passing bow to conservation, saying of course they don't want all the grizzlies killed, but I suspect, if their true impulses were augmented, that would mean the end of Old Ephraim and with him the finest living reminder of pioneer times in the nation.

"The Rocky Mountain Front: One Man's Religion" is the most recent Guthrie article to be published, appearing in the September/October 1987 issue of Montana Magazine.

THE ROCKY
MOUNTAIN FRONT

I am a resident, you might almost say a product, of the Rocky Mountain Front, "the Front," as we have come to call it. It is a strip of land just east of the Continental Divide and includes an edge of the plains, the higher benchlands, the foothills and then the great, jagged wall of the mountains. It starts just east of Glacier Park and includes on its outer rim the towns of Browning, Dupuyer, Bynum, Augusta, and Helena. The crow-flight distance is about 160 miles.

When we speak of the Front we are thinking not of the towns and the plains but of the western rises, the benches, the hills and the mountains that seem to stand guard over creature and land.

I know the Front well, particularly that section west of Choteau, where the Muddy and the Teton and Deep Creek flow, for I spent my young life in the town. I live now 25 miles to the west of it. Just four miles from our home rears my vision site of Ear Mountain. I use the term by extension. It was to the mountain that young Indian boys came, staying on top of it without food or water until, feverish and fanciful, they found their talismans, or medicine, in the form of bird or animal, thereafter held sacred. Don't think of them as foolishly superstitious. Superstition, as a philosopher remarked, is the other fellow's religion. I find my medicine just by looking.

Again to the west of us, three miles or less, runs the Old North Trail, which, it is surmised, travelers from Siberia followed after crossing the Bering land bridge to Alaska. One theory is that they merged with or became our American Indians. Well, maybe. Another is that they continued on to South America. Maybe again. The truth lies centuries beyond the backward reach of history. But there is no question that man came down the Front.

The trail is just one evidence of prehistory to be found on the Front. In late years 10 miles from our place, paleontologists have uncovered thousands of fossils of duck-billed dinosaurs—those of adults, infants, nests and eggs, all vestiges of the life of 70 million years ago. It perished, that life, seemingly all at once. Scientists incline to the belief that a great asteroid struck the earth and that the animals died from the dust and debris and especially from the cold that came with the blotting out of the sun. They wonder, too, about the classification of dinosaurs. They are commonly called reptiles, but the evidence suggests they were warm-blooded creatures that cared for their young, as reptiles are not and do not.

After the dinosaur came the mammal, notably the buffalo that included the Front in its range. If it weren't for obstacles in the way of sight, I could see a buffalo jump from our home. The bottom of that jump, where Indians butchered the dead and dying, has been mined and screened for arrowheads and mined and screened again, for it has been a rich source.

At the age of 86, living on the Front, I have come to feel a part of what has gone before, kin to dinosaur and buffalo and departed Indians that lived here. When I step out of doors and hear a small crunch underfoot I sometimes suspect I may be treading on the dusted bones of duckbill or bison or red man killed in the hunt.

But as I am part and brother of what went before, so am I related to the living creatures that inhabit the Front. They exist in great variety. That fact struck me again this past July when my wife Carol and I were returning from a meeting up the Teton canyon. It was night, but the long light of summer held on, and there in the middle of the road, magical, a mountain lion paused, then glided across into the bushes. A mountain lion! A creature so shy of man, so elusive, as to be rarely seen. Sometime travelers in the mountains hereabouts have never spotted one.

To find mountain lions you need dogs, and one day, I fear, hunters' dogs will find the scent of this one and tree it after a chase, and the hunters, following, will shoot it down and get their proud pictures in the paper along with their trophy.

I count out animals in my mind—bears, black and grizzly, deer, coyotes, badgers, beavers, raccoons, otters, minks, skunks, ground squirrels, three kinds of rabbit, sometimes an elk, rarely a wolf, maybe a moose, more rarely a mountain lion. An experienced guide once told me that the Front, at least part of the time, was home to virtually every Rocky Mountain creature.

Of these, bears get the most attention, particularly grizzly bears. The black bear is quite common and almost always harmless, and so people accept it, more or less. In our 12 years here, two have nosed around the house, hoping for garbage that we don't leave outside. The grizzly is a different proposition. Alarmed suddenly, chased or in the presence of imagined danger to its cubs, it is a fearsome animal.

Some people have criticized me for defending the grizzly. How wrong-headed was I to overlook the danger and discount the losses? All right. The passions of the moment pass and don't count in the long run. I stand by my convictions while tending to forget and forgive.

But while thinking of that great bear, the most memorable creature alive on this continent, this part of our lore and our heritage, I don't want it to disappear. Let him live.

Our visitors, in addition to the two black bears, include a badger. It ambles around the house, intent on some business of its own, and, unafraid, takes its flowing body down the bank to the river and is lost to sight. Deer are frequent presences in our backyard. Coyotes often sing at night. Once Carol spotted a wolf.

We are hosts now to five cottontails, a mixed blessing since they eat the plants in our ground-level flower boxes. We threaten to shoot them, but don't. Our impulses are contradictory. Last winter we heard a cry, that seldom-uttered, plaintive cry of the desperate, and we hurried to the back window to see. A cottontail was jumping, jumping to dislodge a little white death that swung from its neck. But no jumps could loosen that throat hold. The rabbit fell down and quivered and died, and the little white death fed on its blood. And our sympathies were with the pesky rabbit, not with the weasel.

The Bob Marshall Wilderness just west of the Front is great and needs no justification other than its being wilderness. Horseback riders and backpackers penetrate the miles of it to their great enjoyment. But what far more visitors see and appreciate is the Front. They come to it to picnic, to fish and to hunt and perhaps just to breathe the breath of free space. They can reach it easily, for there are roads to many spots. Men and women, residents of the Front towns and of the bigger ones farther east, come in numbers.

The situation may change. Some of the Front is privately owned. Far more is under the control of the Bureau of Land Management and the Forest Service. Much hinges on their decisions, for oil men and miners and timber cutters keep filing for permission to drill and blast and cut. In one instance I know of, drillers didn't wait for clearance. Activities like these frighten wild animals away, deface the land and in the case of timber felling give rise to floods.

Officials of counties like my own tend to line up with the despoilers, not without immediate reason, for counties are hard put these days, suffering from two years of dry weather and low prices for cattle and grains. Anything at all promising in the way of cash and jobs exerts its appeal. I believe, if reluctantly, that the officials are reflecting the convictions of the constituents.

They forget. They forget. As one man said of the Forest Service, they have no memory function. Without remembrance of the past, they are compelled to repeat it, as the philosopher Santayana said of history and civilizations. Few remember when the Teton River ran full, season to season. That was before clear-cutting and overgrazing and cultivation made a spring flood of it and a dry creek bed later.

Real estate developers threaten us, too. They regard every open space that may yield profit as an invitation to hammer and saw. Given opportunity and customers they would develop all the miles of the Front. That would be the end of it, of course.

We who live near the mountains tend to be protective of our environment. When it was proposed to sell cabin sites on about 150 acres along the south fork of the Teton, we filed suit. By we I mean ourselves, the Kenneth Gleasons, and the Wilderness Society. A few contributors helped us. The cabin sites, 37 of them, lay at an important entrance to the Bob Marshall Wilderness.

We proved in court that the contour of the acreage prevented effective septic disposal. We proved that the likelihood of finding water was remote. We proved that the State Board of Health, one of the defendants, had hardly investigated at all before giving the development approval.

Unaccountably, the judge, after accepting our contentions, found for the defendants.

We prepared to appeal and went so far as to have a transcript made. We didn't win the case then, so much as wear it out. Facing an appeal, the developers gave up, so advised, I would bet, by their attorneys who felt that a reversal was sure.

It may sound as if I oppose every would-be cabin builder, as if, given the power, I would close the Front to all cabin seekers. That is not my position and not, I am sure, the position of other dwellers here. What's a cabin here and there, reasonably insulated by space? But 37 cabins on limited acreage! One building to about every four acres! Suburban cluster in our foothills!

I have fished most of the streams of the Front. I have hunted its covers for rabbits and grouse. From its beaver basins and lakes I have flushed mallards and bluebills, three kinds of teal and other waterfowl I made sure to identify. I have picnicked with family and friends. I have known all its weathers—the caress of spring, the frying heat of summer and the bite of cold when sundogs dog the sun. I can't say, with the naturalist John Burroughs, that always have goodness and joy waited on my comings and goings. It's enough that I have come out ahead.

I suppose people not of the Front think it odd of us, or at least eccentric, to live where we do, away from cities and the offerings of cities, away even from a small town where we could have close neighbors and take part in community activities. Maybe we are a bit strange, but I look to the north and the south, where foothills rise, east to the great roll of the high plains and west to the mountains and my vision site of Ear Mountain, and good medicine lies all around.

This text is taken verbatim from Guthrie's autobiography, The Blue Hen's Chick: A Life in Context, *where it appeared as the closing chapter. In March of 1965—the same year in which the autobiography was published—the piece also saw print, under the title "An April in Montana," in* Holiday *magazine. Just as this highly personal essay made an appropriate finale for* The Blue's Hen's Chick, *so it seems a fitting conclusion to this otherwise chronological collection of Guthrie's socio-environmental essays.*

AN

APRIL IN

MONTANA

Why, if my gaze is even half focused, do I choose to live in a state of which I'm critical in the directions I've mentioned? As I start to count the becauses, I become fidgety. Maybe a writer should not come to terms with his environment. Maybe he writes more and better in recalled happiness, away from what pleases him, present only in retrospect. Elsewhere I might have worked harder; elsewhere, where I might have felt homesick, deprived and forlorn, I might have reached farther. In almost ten years I haven't done much. A stint or two in Hollywood. In a series of novels one book, *These Thousand Hills*—which was my most difficult and least successful because it dealt with the cowpuncher and had to avoid, if it could, the stylized Western myth. A collection of short stories [*The Big It*, Houghton Mifflin, 1969]. A handful of magazine pieces. Less than a handful of verses.

I haven't worked hard enough and advance as excuse, as most writers do with some justice, that I don't know when I'm working. If I get stuck on a page, the way out may come to me while I'm shaving.

The question stands: Why am I here?

I like Montana, and I like Montanans. Most of my people, aside from their certain rigidities, are agreeable and generous and in person engaging. The rancher in a pickup stops to ask if he can help you with a flat. The old-timer, his youth renewed by hundred-proof, talks of his friend, the history of just yesterday. The moneyed man plays poker with his barber and asks him home to take pot luck. So it's been a bad year? What the hell? Another season's coming up. The bartender, just presented to a giant of a man, says cordially, "Jesus Christ! You're big enough to eat hay." The chambers of commerce, confusing size with quality, can still brag of the fish and game that only uncongestion can account for.

Time and adjustment and liking and my sense of context. The mind-heard echoes of old trappers on the beavered streams. The grind of prairie schooners. A buffalo skull in a wallow. The time-gentled melancholy of the first homesteaders, forced to leave the sunsets. An arrowhead shining in the gravel after rain. All these and more.

Mountain water over shining rock, which DeVoto said he loved the best of all. Stars like bonfires. Clouds swelling in the bellies of the peaks in Glacier Park. A cottontail at the edge of a thicket. A horseman and a bronc. Old Chief Big Lake's grave on a benchland facing westward over the valley of the Teton. Fishing streams and one trout rising to my Royal Coachman, and my not caring much if it should get away. A bar of song remembered from some country schoolhouse dance. The wild geese V-ing, shouting their adventure. A buck's antlers through the quaking asp. The first men here and the things they saw that I see now. The coyotes calling.

A different, a less harried, a more open and a better world. My world?

April in Montana is a harsh and fretful month, a time of wayward winds and unpredicted snows and rains as cold as snow. If the sun shines for a day or two or three, the eager willows swell, and sap warms the wintered aspens in the foothills, and magpies start building nests like twiggy basketballs—but all too early, all too soon. Snow will come again, and cold, and the reaching grasp at new life be discouraged and postponed. Ordinarily, that is.

It is the last of April, and we have just had a big snow which, after a dry winter, is good for grass and wheat but bad for birds and buds. Even now there is a touch of storm in the air, and the sun, after trying to shine, seems ready to give up.

I am at Twin Lakes, looking more often out a quart-sized picture window than at this waiting page. The place is a pocket in the great eastern apron of the Rockies, and I have kept the unimaginative name, not wanting to monkey with history even if I could persuade people to indulge my monkeyshines.

I am alone, but when I look down at the floor I see my old dead dog again. She hates cold and misty-moist weather and gazes up with pleading eyes, knowing I am God and could change things if I would. I dislike to disappoint her. All gods must feel regretful.

It is good to be alone, though lonely, while the fire in the old range crackles and gladdens bones as furnace fires and fanned electric heat cannot. It is good to think, to sit and think or just to think you're thinking, to let come to mind what will—convictions, fancies, the bigs and littles of experience and fragments of a dance tune danced to long ago. And here you are, the product of what has gone before; yet not all of it can account for the you that you've become. And yet, I think, and not for nothing altogether: the blue hen's chick.

A few days more, and I shall wish for people and routine and someone to do the dishes, but now I find release in living as I please, alone, erratic and untidy, and in working as I please, with books and papers and unanswered letters scattered around me and discarded pages under foot. I have a hunch that all clean desks have littered drawers. It is good to be away from noise and the barbiturate temptation of TV, to be free of outside rule and expectation. Internal fret is fret enough.

Outside, the snow is melting but the sky still overcast. Clouds obscure Ear Mountain, but I know it rises there, four miles away, and on brighter days will bolster me again. The green grass shows on the shoveled path beyond the window, and birds are feeding on the grain that I have scattered. Now is the season of the junco, the Oregon snowbird. In sight are some two dozen of them, perky little creatures, smaller than English sparrows, with dark hoods pierced by white beaks and marks of rusty red on backs and sides. They arrive to feed as if on signal and on signal wing away, shortly to return together. Something about the window keeps confusing them as it does not other birds. Four or five have hit it, leaving bits of down on the glass, and one lay shut-eyed and gasping afterwards. I went out and picked him up and brought him in and, though confident of his identity, checked him against my key to birds. In an hour he got his breath and vision and fluttered hot-pulsed in my palm and on release set out uncertainly.

A yellowheaded blackbird, a rare sight at this altitude, just made a landing on the path, brilliant in his gold and ebony against the farther snow. Out toward the woodpile six or seven magpies are shouting grace for fare left there. A solitary chipmunk munches something on the fence rail. I cannot see the home lake from my makeshift desk but know a greenhead and a lady mallard are making love off shore and that a goldeneye, resplendent for his courting, cruises with his mate.

We shall have young life around the place again this year. Not only ducklings. Magpies, the smartest of our birds. White-crowned sparrows. Pine squirrels. Flickers. Clark's nutcrackers. Every season squirrels and flickers fight for homes in one old hollow aspen. Hard to say which side will win. Sometimes one does, sometimes the other. Already the great horned owls that like the north lake have hatched their broods. Perhaps I should say brood, for I don't know that more than one pair nests there. One pair does, though, and has for year on year—the only Twin Lakes birds to mate before the Ides of March.

Cottontails a cup would cover will explore our world, their eyes fluid with wonder, and a doe will lead her fawn to a salt block on the hill, and in the early mornings the marmots will be out. The tramp black bear of last year may recommence his rounds. With luck we'll see a mountain lion. No sweat. We go unmolested, without arms.

Interruption.

I just shot a skunk.

I'm always glad of interruptions. They take me from the typewriter, and I find excuses for not coming back. Well, tomorrow will be another day and, from the looks of things, one like today.

The skunk—a male, I think, but, male or female, not an it because animals aren't its to one withdrawn from human company—he came poking round the woodpile, nosing for the scraps that I had left for magpies. When I went out he spread his black and white and stomped his front feet, warning that he'd pivot and perfume me if I dared another step. At my retreat he ambled off with fine contempt, poised possessor of world power. I put shells in my 20-gauge and followed him and shot. Usually a skunk, dying, releases a defiant charge. This one didn't. With all his powers he fell and lay, his farewell to the world unfired.

Not until late years did skunks invade my country. We had assumed we were too high for them. They came, though, perhaps as a consequence of great increases lower down. I incline to think their thriving may be due in part to the proud war waged on coyotes by experts of the state and nation, for there is evidence that coyotes, though daunted by grown skunks, still feast on those newborn.

A skunk is more than a nuisance, to watch for in the dark, to call your pup away from if you can. An egg- and chick-eater, he is the first destroyer of ground chickens. Give him free rein, and larks and sparrows, prairie chickens, pheasants, grouse and even ducks will thin out and maybe disappear. That he is a mouser, too, is not atonement for his sins.

The animals I trap or shoot or poison I kill reluctantly, in the hard knowledge that I should or must.

Take the noisome little clown, the pack or trade rat. Once inside your cabin—and he'll get there if you don't watch all openings, including the dampers on your stove—he'll wreak havoc while, with merry thumps of tail, he beats out his vandal's glee. He'll soil, he'll chew, he'll steal, he'll hide his loot and leave behind a stench impervious to all the vaunted hosts of cleansers and deodorants.

I can say nothing for the porcupine except, when I consider his figure and fecundity, that love indeed must conquer all. He's stupid. He's destructive. He thrashes his cruelly needled tail without discrimination, into the faces of dogs, who go insane with pain and fury, and against the velvet noses of merely curious calves and colts and often older livestock. Unattended, the quills may strike the brain or central nervous system, for they are feathered to work deep. First, though, unable to suckle or to graze for the stubbled torture in their muzzles, ranch animals may starve unless detected, locked in a squeeze and operated on with pliers. Some great authority will have to tell me how porcupines contribute to nature's equilibrium.

Pack rats and porcupines and skunks—these I destroy, and one other creature that I hate to most of all. That is the beaver.

I see him every summer, for he keeps insisting that my premises are his. I see the quiet V he wedges in the lake at sundown. I hear the hard smack of his tail as, startled, he submerges. I spot him on the shore, braced by his tail, chipping at a lovely aspen with teeth like sharp and highly tempered chisels. I see his winter store of severed saplings, set under water in the mud close by his house. I see and, seeing, know this gentle creature will have to be removed.

Given less time than even I with my experience can think, he'll lay waste an aspen grove. A neurosis afflicts him. Like the human layers-waste of forests, though with more mystic motivation, he has to be logging, whether downed trees serve the purpose of food or dams or not. He has to be as busy as a beaver and, under this compulsion, is as dedicated as any bureaucrat. More, like the Corps of Engineers or the brass of Reclamation, he can't endure the sight of running water. So he clogs not only streams, with sometime benefit, but irrigation ditches that, dammed, could never contribute to power or navigation. Ten times or more a summer he crams his cuttings in the round-holed headgate that lets a ditch into my lake, though not the best of dams there would create a pond. It is enough for him, an engineer, that he slow or stop the flow.

But still I like to watch him and feel poorer when I shoot him or take him from a trap.

It used to be the animals and I had privacy. Eight hundred acres, no matter that they're poor, provided range enough. We could roam and run and take a dip, knowing that the sky, eccentric though it might be, was free of peering eyes. Now planes spy on us and take pictures, I suppose, always by my impression when the human hiker halts his steps on nature's orders and stands or squats exposed; and their drone in any case is alien and unwelcome, remindful of the fact that progress leaves us no retreat. Not often but too often they are Forest Service planes and private kites; and yesterday there came a jet. So perfected that it can't work up a sweat within the speed of sound, it broke the barrier with its synthetic thunderclap and upset the animals and me and shook the bones of this old cabin, which seemed to me to whimper all night long while the west wind tried to soothe it. Old things ought not to be shook up. Price of survival, the smooth brass of the Air Force tells us smoothly.

The jet cleaved the air, leaving against the unoffending sky the white cut of its swipe. I watched it out of sight, hoping it would fall on a scientist.

In a wild moment once I undertook to underscore, by means of a hillbilly song, my hoary and admittedly excessive attitude. This humdinger was to be the cry of a mountain man like me—who wanted space and air, but folks moved about, and as folks do they bred a crew till only the air was bare.

Hiatus here because, after this infirm beginning or something close to it, I skipped the next and connecting verse and, under a strong wind, sailed into the chorus. It went this way:

Keep them jaybirds outta my sky,
Where only birds was meant to fly,
And the Lord on High
Says you're coming too nigh.
Keep them noisy, nosey, pyznus jimcracks
Outta my sky!

At this point I decided the task was beyond my talents, and, anyhow, my case was long since lost.

Better than drawing boards, test flights and test explosions, I like the military preparations said to have been pursued by a loser in the Riel or Cree Rebellion up north in Canada some eight decades past. He slipped across the line into Montana and with him somehow slipped nine squaws. His intention: to breed a family fighting force so numerous as to right the wrong. Of course the war was never waged, but the man tried mightily, so mightily that hereabouts and nowadays a man can hardly number the fruits of his endeavors.

Gazing out the window toward my fence line, I feel a twinge, residual from history and myth, because I don't raise something here, but let Nature take her course instead. Not much of this rock-and-jackpine country recommends itself for cultivation, but there's a spot or two where hardy garden stuff would grow if the grower fenced and garrisoned the garden against sneak attacks by cottontails and black-tailed deer and mountain gophers. But I'd rather walk than hoe, rather recognize wild flowers than weed tame turnips. Coral root, an orchid of a sort, rises colored in the aspen grove, like asparagus with apoplexy, and Indian paintbrush blows, and on the flats in season the yellow loco lifts its deep-piled carpet above the modest carpet of the carpet flowers. And I delight in knowing among what I'm cast, delight in surely saying this plant is this, that animal that, and here a deer survived its journey through the night.

But still the sturdy yeoman, who plows not but only watches and from time to time puts labored words on paper. Who asks not for handouts either, for growing or not growing. What did happen to yesterday's stout yeoman?

A new arrival, a redpoll, not so jaunty as the juncos, feeds with them on the path, feeds unafraid and unmolested, his Roman red respected. And two bronze grackles, male and female, lower flaps and come to earth. No jolts. No taxiing. Perfect, runless, two-point landings. Unconcerned with other birds, they peck and preen. One preens, that is. The male, not yet allowed by her to sow, reaps a tame oat and then extends his wings and spreads his tail and flutters all his feathers and, that display done, cocks his white eyes at the sky as if asking heaven when. The show-off ritual, the beginning ritual of love.

Idly, while I've watched, I've wondered what I want, where I stand and what's my doctrine. A simple answer came, though the years have taken part of its fulfillment.

To lean but, more important, to be leaned on,

For that's what friendship's for.
To be loved but to love,
Or what's the use?
To be generous toward life,
Else I lose myself.
Above all else, to care!

Suddenly the yard is bare, abandoned by the birds, left vacant at the last by the chipmunk after he had flirted goodnight from the woodpile, and I feel deserted and thrown in on myself, as if I were the last of life.

Westward, astride the backbone of the Rockies, the sun sets through the mist. Time to have a drink. To have two, maybe. Almost time, as old-time camp cooks used to say, to burn a mulligan.

End of an April day.

POSTSCRIPT

In the fall of 1987, *Four Miles from Ear Mountain*, a collection of 23 of A. B. Guthrie, Jr.'s poems, several having conservation themes, was published in a limited edition by the Kutenai Press of Missoula, Montana. Additionally, the indefatigable writer has yet another novel in the works, continues to publish poetry and magazine pieces, makes occasional public appearances and is in the process of expanding and updating his autobiography.

A

GUTHRIE

BIBLIOGRAPHY

Some of A. B. Guthrie, Jr.'s books are still available in hardcover from the original publishers. Several have been reprinted in various softbound editions (most recent paperback publishers are indicated in parentheses in the listing below), while others are out of print and to be found only in libraries, private collections and, occasionally, on the shelves of quality used-book stores. Among those titles now out of print, several original editions are highly prized among collectors. Aside from obvious titles such as *The Big Sky*, included among the collectibles—because, Guthrie says, of its scarcity rather than its literary quality—is his little-known first novel, *Murders at Moon Dance*, which, in 1987, was valued in excess of $150 in original hardcover.

Murders at Moon Dance. E. P. Dutton, 1943; a paperback edition, also out of print, carries the altered title of *Trouble at Moon Dance.*

The Big Sky. Sloane, 1947; rights subsequently purchased by Houghton Mifflin (Bantam).

The Way West. Sloane, 1949; rights subsequently purchased by Houghton Mifflin (Bantam).

These Thousand Hills. Houghton Mifflin, 1956 (Bantam).

The Big It. Houghton Mifflin, 1960 (Ballantine); an anthology of short stories.

The Blue Hen's Chick. McGraw-Hill, 1965; autobiographical.

Arfive. Houghton Mifflin, 1970 (Bantam).

Wild Pitch. Houghton Mifflin, 1973.

Once Upon A Pond. Mountain Press, 1973; for children.

The Last Valley. Houghton Mifflin, 1975 (Bantam).

The Genuine Article. Houghton Mifflin, 1977.

No Second Wind. Houghton Mifflin, 1980.

Fair Land, Fair Land. Houghton Mifflin, 1982.

Playing Catch-Up. Houghton Mifflin, 1985.

ACKNOWLEDGMENTS

No writer or editor can assemble a chronicle of another person's life and work without the cooperation and assistance of a great many others. Sources quoted throughout Part I and in the editor's introductions to the individual Guthrie essays in Part II are cited as they occur in the text. The origin and publication history of each of the 22 essays in the collection are cited in the individual introductions. Additionally, the editor acknowledges special debts to the following persons, publications and organizations:

Senator Max Baucus and the staff of his Helena, Montana, and Washington, D.C., offices for making available Guthrie's 1985 Senate testimony in behalf of the grizzly bear.

Mr. Ingvard Henry Eide for permission to reprint an excerpt from Guthrie's introduction to Eide's superb book of photographs, *American Odyssey: The Journey of Lewis and Clark.*

Carol Guthrie for invaluable support and criticism during the research, preparation and editing of the manuscript.

Houghton Mifflin Company, Boston, for granting permission to quote at length from Guthrie's novels, to which they hold rights.

Dr. Charles E. Hood, Jr., dean of the School of Journalism, University of Montana, Missoula, for making available and allowing quotation from his exhaustive, unpublished master's thesis, *Hard Work and Tough Dreaming: A Biography of A. B. Guthrie, Jr.* (1969).

Bill Marshall, Claire McCann, and the staff (including an unnamed graduate assistant) at the University of Kentucky Library, Special Collections and Archives for providing various editorials written while Guthrie was an editor for the *Lexington Herald-Leader*.

The Bob Marshall Foundation, Kalispell, Montana, for permission to quote from their provocative film *A Path to America's Wilderness*.

Gary McLean, forest archaeologist for the Flathead National Forest, for friendly cooperation in making vital connections and providing valuable quotations and resource materials.

Montana Magazine and its editor, Carolyn Cunningham.

Montana: The Magazine of Western History and Chris Eby for providing resource materials from their archives.

Parade Magazine and its managing editor, Larry Smith.

Willis G. Regier, director, University of Nebraska Press, for sound advice and candid criticism.

The Writer magazine, for making available Guthrie's 1949 article, *Characters and Compassion*.

ABOUT
THE
EDITOR

David L. Petersen lives with his wife Carolyn in the San Juan Mountains 15 miles northeast of Durango, Colorado, from where he writes and edits as senior editor West for *Mother Earth News* magazine. He holds degrees in social sciences and creative writing, and is an occasional visiting professor of English at Fort Lewis College in Durango. Petersen has also written seven nonfiction children's books (Childrens Press), as well as *Building the Traditional Hewn-Log Home* (Mother Earth News Books, 1987), and *Among the Elk,* with photographs by Alan D. Carey (Northland Press, 1988).